New Glass Architecture

New Glass Architecture
Brent Richards
Photographs by Dennis Gilbert

Laurence King Publishing

Published in 2006 by
Laurence King Publishing Ltd
71 Great Russell Street
London WC1B 3BP
T +44 (0)20 7430 8850
F +44 (0)20 7430 8880
enquiries@laurenceking.co.uk
www.laurenceking.co.uk

Text and design © Laurence King Publishing

A catalogue record for this book is available from
the British Library

ISBN-13: 978 1 85669 376 9
ISBN-10: 1 85669 376 7

Designed by Atelier Works

Managing Editor Mark Fletcher
Proofreader Tessa Clark
Indexer Sue Farr

Printed in China

Page 2 Trees reflected in the glass wall of the
Fondation Cartier in Paris designed by Jean
Nouvel (1994).

Contents

Space, Light and Transformation

Reference

Case studies

Glass family tree

The 'glass family tree' shares the common foundation of a glass architecture that started with the Crystal Palace in 1851. The tree traces a growing movement of 'constructing with light' – projects that relate to the sensorial and emotional attributes of the material, rather than the functional and technological features of modern architecture. This movement first emerged in the 1930s, became important in the 1990s, and in the new Millennium is becoming increasingly significant.

Buildings in bold are featured as case studies in this book.

6

Year	Transparency	Space	Opacity
1851		**Crystal Palace** London	
1855–1856	Gardner's Stores, Glasgow		
1864–1865	Oriel Chambers, Liverpool		
1865–1867	Galleria Vittorio Emanuele, Milan		
1898	Gage Stores, Chicago		
1903–1911	Carson PS Stores, Chicago		
1903–1911	Steiff Works, Giengen		
1903–1905	La Samaritaine Store, Paris		
1904–1906			Post Office, Vienna
1911	Fagus Works, Alfed-an-der-Leine		
1914			Werkbund Pavilion, Cologne
1919–1922	German Pavilion, Barcelona		
1929–1930	Tugendhat House, Brno		
1930	Villa Savoye, Paris		
1931–1932			Maison de Verre, Paris
1946–1951	Farnsworth House, Illinois		
1949	Glass House, New Canaan		
1951		Notre Dame Chapel, Ronchamp	
1954–1958	Seagram Building, New York		
1971–1975	Willis Faber & Dumas, Ipswich		
1980	Goldstein House, Beverley Hills		
1982	Renault Centre, Swindon		
1986	Sculpture Pavilion, Sonsbeek		
1986			Lloyds Building, London
1987		Arab Institute, Paris	
1990	Louvre Pyramid, Paris		
1990	Video Gallery, Groningen		
1991			Kunsthaus, Bregenz
1992		**Shaw Offices, New York**	
1993		**Kiasma Museum, Helsinki**	
1994	**Broadfield House, Dudley**	**Fondation Cartier, Paris**	**Goetz Collection, Munich**
1997	Villa de L'eau du Verre, Atami	**Museum of Art, Lille**	**Concert Hall, St Pölten**
1997		**Chapel of Ignatius, Seattle**	
1998	**Innovation Centre, Majorca**		**Museum Het Valkhof, Nijmegen**
1999			**Kursaal Centre, San Sebastian**
2000	Pavilion Collegeverre, Rheinback		
2001	**British Museum, London**	**Condé Nast Café, New York**	**Colorium, Düsseldorf**
2001	**Skywood House, London**	**DZ Bank, Berlin**	**Sendai Médiathèque, Sendai**
2001	**Kimmel Center, Philadelphia**		
2002		**City Hall, Alphen aan den Rijn**	**Laminata House, Leerdam**
2003			**Laban Dance Centre, London**

Year	Transparency	Colour/Pattern/Luminescence	Opacity
2004	**30 St Mary Axe, London**	**Kunsthaus, Graz**	**Torre Agbar, Barcelona**
2004		Prada, Tokyo	
2004		Dior, Tokyo	
2004		Louis Vuitton LVMH, New York	

Foreword

'The task of architecture is to make visible how the world touches us … through vision, we touch the stars and the sun.' (Maurice Merleau-Ponty, 1994)

Historically, the transparency of glass has provoked an almost mystical response and a fascination with the material's unique properties as a versatile and spectacular substance – one that literally illuminates buildings and brings to life the polemic nature of architecture itself. Latterly, the use of glass in contemporary architecture has been associated with the functional pursuit of lighter construction and the creation of the minimal envelope. It is treated essentially as a 'non-material', utilized to capture space and define spatial volumes but increasingly devoid of a representative architectural language or detail.

The conceptual basis for much of modern architecture has been generated through using glass to create the minimal building structure, to extol the notion of lightweight construction solutions, as the simple multipurpose envelope, and to permit the maximum penetration of light into the building's interior. Paradoxically, glass buildings are frequently heavy rather than light, and the structural demands they make are onerous to the inexperienced designer.

However, it is only in the last 15 years, that the full potential of a glass architecture has begun to be fully revealed and realized, as a new language of light, spatiality and conscious dematerialization has begun to be possible. This reading of an independent glass architecture – while imagined in the minds of many, from Paul Scheerbart, Bruno Taut and Pierre Chareau to Mies van der Rohe (it was particularly evident in Paul Scheerbart's 1914 books *Glass Architecture* and *The Grey Cloth,* the latter a novel about glass architecture) – is significant in its recognition of the potential of glass to challenge the transformation of materiality and to provide a new paradigm. This paradigm has emerged with increasing coherence since 1990, realized as an alternative expressiveness to that of the minimal envelope, and reborn out of a holistic resolution of glass technology itself.

This book sets out to demonstrate that a new aesthetic that has been developing apace in glass architecture since the 1990s can, in fact, be directly traced back to the erection of the Crystal Palace in 1851. It is therefore necessary to reconsider the family tree of glass architecture (*see opposite*), not as a singular, highly engineered technological heritage or a linear history of a sophisticated material interface, but rather as an architecture in which glass is used in a creative sense, to exploit the material qualities of glass for its spatiality and to depict an experiential syntax of architectural expression. The central premise of this book is the distinction made between the modern movement's pursuit of the 'lightness of construction' and contemporary architecture's investigation of the potential for 'constructing with light', as a means to dematerialize the structure through the use of luminosity.

'The void itself becomes the raw material for knowing the possibility of being.'
Francesco Dal Co on Tadao Ando

Notions of Space and Spatiality

Our preoccupation with space has a long history. It is central to our human condition and sense of well-being. Space, and the use of space as in its qualitative condition, are both integral to our inner harmony. Spatial qualities lie in the existential awareness of light and dark, in the openness and concealment of function, as well as in the beauty of space as expressed in emptiness (the Japanese express this profound state as *wabi*).

Glass, as a building material, offers a special interlayer between our outer and inner space, and has opened up and contained, as well as sheltered and revealed, the architecture of its time. Architects' pursuit of the minimal environmental envelope has created an evolutionary and reductionist approach, whereby glass has become a predominant and essential cladding material of contemporary architecture.

In particular, new developments in glass technology have enabled it to be utilized as a complete structural material, through the use of special films, glues and coatings. Subsequently, the notion of spatial design has become more significant, and, when successfully articulated, defines an innovative art in its own right. This approach has involved the treatment of space as matter, and a move away from the creation of solid forms, shells, envelopes and the engineered language of structure. It has permitted the potential for buildings

to have depth, discovery, mystery and shadow, to be truly multisensory, to be a multifaceted experience of the metaphysical. In the words of the Japanese designer Isamu Noguchi: 'There is a feeling of time having stopped, of an infinity of winds having weathered, and left a shell ….'

But these qualities are not present just in the articulation of the material characteristics of glass, but also in the understanding and the use of space and light, the appreciation of space as a memory of form, and its future merit and vast potential. Through the better appreciation of the representation of glass, it is possible to retrace the roots of glass in architecture, not just as a unique alchemical material, but as a medium that interfaces between worlds: connecting art and science, innovation and enterprise, through human ingenuity from the ancient past to the present and the future.

The key problem for an 'architecture of glass' is that a total use of the material challenges the very heart of its evolutionary transcendence, from aperture to structural envelope, from structure to skin, from skin to transparency and from transparency to lightness. While transparency and lightness reinforce its design possibilities, there are a myriad technical and conceptual challenges to both design and construction. Structure, detailing and environmental controls call for specific solutions, while the design challenge in terms of architecture is representation and conceptualization. Glass has universally provided the medium for light in architecture; it has allowed for dramatic reinterpretations of space and form, and transformed

architecture into a profound approach to provide 'vistas without, and vistas within' (Frank Lloyd Wright).

But an 'architecture of transparency' has the dilemma of being and of realization. How does it manifest and articulate its existence without a tangible nomenclature to communicate its presence? The concept of transparency as distinct from any physical quality of substance, is less about a definition of clearness than it is about that which is clearly ambiguous. In this state lies the paradox, between the literal and the phenomenal, a continuous dialogue between fact and implication. This in turn produces spatial contradictions within which space becomes constructed, substantial and articulated. Therefore, in essence, it is the 'phenomenology of transparency' that moves the spirit and is, equally, visually seductive and illusory to the eye.

In the eye's field of vision this is experienced as perceptual activity, where space is dematerialized and offers a crystalline translucency that has the capacity to synthesize spatial dimensions. The allure of constructions of light is that, consequentially, they become some of the most enduring of memories, which touch the realms of our perception, emotions, and the effects of time and place. Light falling on the object of architecture does not tell a holistic story; it creates an emergent and transient architecture that playfully draws a veil over architecture's form. The French philosopher Jean Baudrillard's exploration of the architectural object considers the shift of contemporary architecture from the aesthetic towards the 'transaesthetic', within which concepts of hyperreality and virtualization are where the real is fundamentally altered. The gradual

move away from what is tangible and real – to the use of ritual, seclusion, ceremony and seduction in architecture – has produced a variable condition. A 'supernova' of architecture – within which the central solid form of architecture's substance is dematerializing – and a type of decomposition and 'ghost of its own reflection' as cultural form are apparent.

Baudrillard makes the case that post-modern society has lost faith in pure technology, and that in turn architecture, in formulating a response to the 'machine for living in' of modernism, has erupted through deconstruction, the fragmentation of plates and planes, and has produced a state of flux and dynamism. This has systematically dismantled the illusory coherence of modern architecture, and its composition, resulting in a confusion of surface, and the superficial. A type of 'hallucinogenic malfunction' has occurred, which has resonated even more dramatically since 9/11, and the destruction of New York's Twin Towers.

The destruction of these twin metaphors of reflected technology symbolized an end to the technological solution in architecture. We are left to ponder whether it is what was destroyed or the demolition that followed that is the more potent symbol of disappearance. The resultant surface has become the aura of the architecture, the building has disappeared in the transparency of the façade. The architectural conceptualization captures an idea – it is no longer a space or a place, it is purely ephemeral.

The field of architecture is one that emanates from a world of seduction. It is about illusion, and is more than

what we see. It is about enabling a composition of space on a succession of sequences, as a memoryscape of an imposed narrative about space and time. These are means by which architecture generates virtual space and tricks the senses into ways of seeing: to conceive a place and non-place, where a non-place in this sense is a kind of mirage, a kind of apparition.

Towards the Light: From sacred to the secular

From the cave dwelling to the domestic house, from the religious altar to the cathedral, the issues in architecture have always been to control climate, provide comfort and let light into the darkness of an interior space. The interface for all three, and the filter for the light, has been the window; the window is the plane of focus for both the functional and aesthetic qualities of the language of the architecture. Glass permitted the window to fuse into architecture's physical form, to converge with the enclosure, to transmit light as well as to celebrate it.

The role of the window, therefore, has always been a key feature in the articulation of the building's façade. The window is necessary to filter the air, to encounter the light and the sun, and to provide a visual connection, or vista, to the outer landscape and urban context. Its arrangement as a building component was an expression, in its cultural context, of the building's composition. But its role was not restricted to that of an environmental filter between the physical elements; it was also an existential link with the world beyond. Notions of space, transparency, lightness and darkness, solid and void all emanate from this

conceptual boundary between the physical and the metaphysical.

The means to interpolate this boundary was enabled by the specificity of glass, as a material that both defined and encapsulated the relationship between space, light and form – a material that captured the physical properties of shelter, warmth and comfort, as well as providing a potent symbol of the interface between spiritual light and well-being. In metaphorical terms, glass became the means to search for the making of 'sacred space in the enlightenment of the darkness'. The exterior of architecture made manifest the spiritual – as well as worldly power and ambition – while the interior opened up in the exuberance of light.

In the case of the architecture of churches, this was extended to the role of 'religious splendour, enigmatic and magnificent in its brilliance of holy light'. Glass appeared as the preordained material joining the heavens and the earth, illuminating the spatial container within which man was both spectator and participant. However, it was through its repeated usage over 3,000 years (by the Syrians, Greeks, Romans and Venetians) that the material progressively evolved from roughly hewn sheets of transparent rock to the high quality, adaptable, vitrified cladding material that today, in our modern built environment, we take for granted.

The limitation for glass has always been in its production. A unique architectural material, its manufacture was consistently difficult and its cost uniformly high. Working the material, mainly by hand, required a range of craft skills and traditional expertise.

Close proximity to natural resources (sand and water) was necessary to reliably make the material in sufficient quantities and in large enough sizes. Its key attribute was its transparency and colour, but it had to be able to be produced flat. It did not possess good insulating properties or provide a manageable strong construction material, and was always liable to break.

Thus, its long development was related to extraordinary technical feats and craft skills that were heavily guarded by secret trade practices, surrounded by mythology and imbued with alchemic mysticism. This expertise focused as much on the search for thinness, as for transparency, as well as on the need to achieve manufacturing quality and consistency. While it was the Syrians who developed thin sheets to serve as primitive windows, it was the Romans who exploited windows as architectural components (window frames finished with thick green/blue cast glass were used as a form of conservatory for growing vegetables out of season).

Successive experimentation with the chemistry of the glass, to increase its performance and appearance, resulted in new additives being introduced to reduce its melting point and improve durability. The blending of ingredients was largely an imprecise art of recipes; and experiments with fluxes, stabilizers and decolorants led the way to architectural applications. Similarly, the process of production provided a parallel development in conceptual thinking to match the technical mastery of the craft. The evolution of an architectural syntax of openings – light and shade – and the language of scale and proportion, was closely allied to the needs of the window as a key element in architectural vocabulary.

Glass offered protection from the elements, and later it permitted the control of air movement for ventilation. It also defined and described new points of vantage to the world outside.

At the same time the exploitation of coloured glass remained largely a means to embellish religious buildings in order to celebrate the cultural and symbolic significance of faith and reverence. Coloured glass was Byzantine in origin, but thereafter made in Normandy, Burgundy and the Rhineland. Clear (or lightly green-tinted) was coloured glass by adding metallic oxides to the glass melt. Glass was often painted, or arranged in pieces, so that it was aesthetically related to the direct penetration of external light, to reveal the architectural structure and its tactile and surface qualities. Coloured glass was later to re-emerge in Venice, which was ideally situated at the trading hub between European merchants and Middle Eastern caravans. Venice also became the centre for the technique of making mirror glass by applying a layer of tin or mercury to flat northern European glass to produce a reflective backing.

Early sheet glass was made using two basic methods that produced cylinder glass and spun glass, both of which searched for consistency and clarity. Subsequent developments sought larger sizes, utilizing new methods of fixing the glass through the architectural language of northern European Gothic architects. The evolution of clear transparent glass was driven by the gradual migration of glass production from the warm Mediterranean north to France and Germany, around the rivers of the Rhone and Rhine

where wood ash and water were plentiful. In addition, river routes guaranteed transportation and delivery of the materials and the export of the finished product.

The Germans were responsible for changing the earlier craft approach – their term for glass was *glesum*, meaning a transparent material. However, the qualities of pure transparency were still subject to the enlightenment of Gothic architecture. The Gothic period, which lasted 400 years, was an era of tremendous development and activity, for new construction commissioned by the Church and for the ingenuity of new structural solutions to provide for larger volumes to house congregations. The evolution of the Gothic stone arch permitted glass to be utilized as an infilling screen of lightweight material, and glass was used to maximize the northern sunlight to illuminate vast spaces for worship. In turn, this use facilitated the appreciation of light for its properties of luminosity, to lighten the darkness, providing a new synergy between physical practicality and emotional reverence (*see above*).

The desire for sheer transparency remained subservient to the properties of translucency. The role of the window was as 'an illuminator of scripture and religious power', and not as a connection to the real world of the everyday. The glass was revealed as a weightless and glowing surface that literally breathed life into the building's form, as a 'perfectly coherent syntax of structure and glass'.

Through the eventual blending of northern European and Mediterranean approaches, there was a shift in the conceptual approach to structure and enclosure, and with it a new approach to the technology of glass manufacture. In England the rise of the Tudors was fuelled by exploration, colonization and wealth. A period of sustained Elizabethan democratic stability gave rise to a wealthy aristocracy willing to patronize craftsmen and invest in the development of great country houses and palaces.

Notably, Hardwick Hall in Derbyshire (1590–97) by Robert Smythson produced a quite distinct landmark that was described as 'more glass than wall'. Not quite a glass house, its windows represented nearly 50 per cent of the façades' treatment, expressed as a totally integrated element of the architecture. A novel approach in spatiality and light, even by today's standards, Hardwick represents an architectural clarity and presence that belies its historical roots.

In the Low Countries, new public buildings displayed similar techniques. In the Netherlands, window openings were used as a sign of trading wealth on the façades of guildhalls and merchant houses. The integration of windows into the façade inspired Dutch artists of the fifteenth century, such as Jan van Eyck, who utilized the conceptual basis of the window as means 'to give measurable depth in a pictorial space'.

For these artists, the light through windows made for more compelling scene setting, offering complexity of uses and interpretations – the window was exploited both as an artistic frame and to observe the painter's concern with the penetration of light and the interplay of shadows and reflections. However, beyond these aesthetic observations the window's cultural significance was as a true building component in the elevation that was to become the signature of future glass buildings.

After the 1550s, the influence of Renaissance Italian craftsmen was key in changing both the interpretation of glass and its technological base. As the two architectural philosophies blended there was a shift in the conceptual approach to structure and enclosure, and with it changes in the technology applied to glass manufacture. The Renaissance building forms gave rise to a broader syntax, within which glass became less an exclusive material and more a commonplace, high quality one for everyday buildings. Thus the notion, and function, of transparency was spread through the window, as a key building component.

From Venice, Muranese glass artists colonized a number of other major European cities, which led to the internationalizing of glass-making and their skills. But the need for sheets of glass drove quality, production and the industrialization of the craft. Sheet glass was normally spun or cylinder glass; the former allowed for a higher polish but a limited size, the latter was larger but duller. Spun glass was mainly used for Venetian mirror glass, but this was unsuitable for larger mirrors. In London, wealthy clients demanded larger panes of strong polished glass. Meanwhile, in Orleans, France, in 1687, Bernard Perrot developed a unique process for casting and polishing glass. This was to gain the royal warrant from Louis XIV, and in due course led to the château at Saint Gobain becoming a place for glass manufacture (which gave its name to Saint Gobain glass). Significantly, the glass works supplied the royal palace of Versailles, which became one of the most extravagant and influential architectural statements of the late seventeenth century.

The palace of Versailles (1669–85) by Louis Le Vau and Jules Hardouin-Mansart, was notable for its Hall of Mirrors, which exploited the use of plate glass along the main frontage of the building, maximizing light into the interior by amplifying its spatial effect by using an inner elevation of mirrored walls. Versailles was reported to be one of the 'greatest rooms in Europe' and its 'glassy' properties were later imitated in Christopher Wren's apartments at Hampton Court, England, in 1689 and 1696.

However, it was a new technique of glass production – the process of annealing glass – that was to prove to be revolutionary. It provided a simple and economical method for making plates of glass of any size or thickness.

Glass Dreams: Technological progress
Whereas the art of the Gothic era had transformed heavenly light into a metaphorical coloured architectural tent, collected through the window element, the twentieth century would provide a more significant technological transformation, with the properties of glass used in its own right. The pursuit of transparency, reflection, translucency and opacity, together with improvements in the understanding of the material properties of glass, advancement of construction techniques, and new processes and product innovations were to lead to a unique notion of

glass engineering. Glass was no longer defined and confined within the rectangular loadbearing frame of the window, but was considered a 'climatic envelope', a membrane that controlled the environment, encapsulated space and mediated the light.

These new ideals had their roots in three areas that were to converge dramatically at the beginning of the nineteenth century. Namely, the Georgian window; the botanical conservatory; and the emergence of the engineered glass house. But it was the Georgian taste for transparency that led to the development of larger windows and their later application in the botanical conservatory.

In the late sixteenth century, it was understood that south-facing structures encouraged plant growth, and glass was subsequently utilized for 'overwintering' flowers and plants. However, it was the exploration of the world in the same century that led to the later development of conservatories. Initially, they were utilized to house and maintain rare seeds and plants as a sign of wealth. This also encouraged early scientific study and in due course botanical 'conservation' of their intrinsically rare specimens – exotic edible fruits, such as oranges, lemons and pineapples, were particularly prized. A fashion for oranges among the European aristocracy gave rise to a proliferation of these conservatories as 'orangeries'. A notable example is the famous Heidelberg orangery by Salomon de Caus (1620). It housed over 400 trees and provided a beautiful protected environment in winter. The conservatory was dismantled after Easter each year and rebuilt the following September. By the early

eighteenth century the Dutch had developed 'greenhouses' for studying and growing plants in which they made use of solar energy and introduced cooling and ventilation. Orangeries as stylized 'winter gardens' were also fashionable with many English architects such as Wren, Hawksmoor and Vanbrugh. As horticultural knowledge progressed the use of sloping glass roofs for diffusing light internally was introduced.

At the beginning of the seventeenth century, when it was first possible to produce very clear glass, systematic improvements had been made in qualifying the standard chemical formulae for glass compounds. By the eighteenth century German sheet glass had taken over from French cast glass, and in 1838 J.T. Chance invented the 'patent plate' glass that was later used to clad the Crystal Palace, in 1851. The true 'glass house' had emerged at the beginning of the nineteenth century due to wealthy patrons' interest in both horticulture and science. Between 1830 and 1851 this led to an unprecedented period of new architectural innovation. In fact, as the same patrons adopted the conservatory for extensions to their fashionable country houses, the role of design influenced the style of their architectural treatment.

A pioneer of this period, John Claudius Loudon, expounded in *Construction of Hothouses* (1817) that glass houses should be scientifically engineered to meet the analysis of performance and technical resolution of erection. He paved the way for wrought–iron ribs, with the glass laid in as a primitive iron-framed membrane – a 'stressed skin' envelope – to strengthen the whole.

His book generated a great international competition to create ever-larger glass structures. In close succession new projects competed for engineering accolades, including the Jardin des Plantes in Paris by Rohault de Fleury (1833); the Great Conservatory at Chatsworth, Derbyshire, by Joseph Paxton (1836); the Palm House in Bicton, Devon (1820–40); the Palm House, Royal Botanical Gardens, Kew, and the Regent's Park conservatory by Richard Turner and Decimus Burton (1845–48); Turner's Glasnevin conservatory (1846–47) and Héctor Horeau's Jardin d'Hiver in Paris (1848). This trend culminated in 1851 with the Crystal Palace in Hyde Park, London, by Thomas Paxton.

One of the most adventurous examples of this period was the conservatory at Chatsworth, which was 84.4 metres (277 feet) long, 37.5 metres (123 feet) wide and 20.4 metres (67 feet) high. It contained a world of microclimates, exotic birds and fish pools. Just 12 years later, the Jardin d'Hiver was built – it was 91.4 metres (300 feet) long, 54.8 metres (180 feet) wide and 60 metres (197 feet) high, with raised walkways, fountains, cafés and planting centrepieces. But even these achievements were to be dramatically exceeded by the proposals for the Crystal Palace – the site of the Great Exhibition in London, that celebrated products from all over the British Empire.

The revolution that took place in this final decade was very dramatic. Due to its public function the Crystal Palace caught the imagination of the general public and clients alike (*see above*). It was all the more radical because it was designed against the more conventional neoclassical grammar of architects such as Nash and

Schinkel. Ruskin criticized its machine aesthetic in his *Seven Lamps of Architecture*, while Pugin called it a 'glass monster'. A modular building of standardized factory-made components, it was clad in a system of plate glass, with a structure of cast- and wrought-iron trusses, and cast-iron columns. The Crystal Palace projected an architecture of glass in a new light. As Konrad Wachsmann put it: 'From the logic and reason, initiating the spirit of the new technological era, rose a beauty of a kind not previously known …. The Crystal Palace was a work of art.'

The Crystal Palace was the first great 'modern' building. It heralded in the twentieth century with technological speed, extolled Paxton's engineering and management coordination, and was a significant achievement in new-found spatiality. Its cathedral-like proportions proclaimed a new transparency for the architecture of glass. For unlike its ancestors – the Gothic cathedrals – this was a 'lantern of pure light'. Its plan was 564 metres (1,850 feet) long by 139 metres (456 feet) wide, generating an enormous free space of 80,000 square metres (861,040 square feet) that extolled the use of light to dramatically illuminate the interior spaces and its brightly colour-coded structure. These same qualities were to be adopted for national railway stations, markets and enclosed shopping arcades in Milan, Paris, Hamburg, Moscow and London.

Light Waves: Constructing with light

While the Crystal Palace can be considered the key departure point for modernism's infatuation with the 'lightness of construction', it could also be seen as a philosophical fault line when another architectural polemic, that of 'constructing with light', emerged, although it was veiled by the ascendancy of the former. While the latter was more to do with understanding the duplicity of the context (which could be perceived both physically and sensually), after an initial burst of idealism in the early decades of twentieth century this alternative polemic was to be held in a dormant state for over 100 years.

Momentarily the two polemics were in direct competition, concealed only by architecture's struggle into the twentieth century, as glass became the ideal material to symbolize the incoming new democracy, as monarchy gave way to workers and private domains gave way to public spaces. For 40 years after the urban barrel-vaulted roofs of Milan's Galleria Vittorio Emanuele and London's St Pancras Station (both 1865–67), Otto Wagner's intimate Post Office Savings Bank (1904) brought together a steel structure and glass roof and floor in a more direct aesthetic essay on modern materials. The building was also significant as a radical representation of the future role of glass architecture.

In this shift, buildings like this were no longer pure architectural elements – roof, wall or window – but instead single structures. The architecture and the engineering were combined into a singular solution and defined elements in their new glass form were no longer articulated as before. Thus, the absolute quality of glass as a new light-reactive material was idealized – it was 'there and not there'. It was manifested in the abstract, in reflections and transparencies, and in the play of surfaces; it sensationalized the light in space in a sensorial manner.

The turn of the century saw a new idealism and a consciousness of space, time and speed, and this was reflected in a revolution in European arts and culture. In the wake of the Impressionists, and their concern with light and fragmentation, there followed new ideas in paintings by Gris, Braque and Duchamp, who experimented with collage and superimposition using glass. In Marcel Duchamp's *Le Grand Verre* (1923) he explored the use of fragments of glass, reflected imagery, combined with projection and manipulation of the visual image.

The alternative lineage of glass architecture – constructing with light – first developed in a very short period from 1914 to 1932. In this particular period, the writer Paul Scheerbart's utopian call for 'the architecture of glass' was answered by Bruno Taut's Glass Pavilion for the Werkbund Exhibition at Cologne in 1914 and echoed in Mies van der Rohe's designs for an unbuilt scheme for Friedrichstrasse in Berlin (1922). The potential of glass was later realized functionally in Mies's Tugendhat House in Brno, Czechoslovakia (1928–30), and extolled in his German Pavilion at Barcelona (1929). However, it was in Pierre Chareau's Maison de Verre in Paris (1931) that these schemes merged and crystallized into a new formal language that had not been seen before.

This revolution, lasting some 15 years, is possibly the least known, but one of the greatest, sustained 'moments' in twentieth-century glass architecture. It

combined the vision of a future of glass architecture with the experimentation and exploration of the potential of the new polemic, as well as scaling up the crossover to pragmatic building forms. In the Maison de Verre it was an enigmatic blueprint for the future. Collectively these ideals represented a paradigm shift, which later was to be restrained only by the inability of the glass industry to produce large enough glass sheets. (Curtain walling was first developed in 1954, but not commercially available until the early 1960s.)

The principal breakthrough was Bruno Taut's Glass Pavilion (*see above*). It is considered very much the precursor of an active revolution to initiate a new architectural culture beyond the Crystal Palace's technical innovation, towards how design can add to the quality of life. Taut's profound interest in a new utopian glass architecture was the culmination of an early dialogue with Paul Scheerbart. In 1914, in *Architecture of Glass*, Scheerbart wrote: 'Our culture is a product of our architecture. In order to raise our culture to a higher level, we are forced, whether we like it or not, to change our architecture …. This, however, we can only do by introducing a glass architecture, which admits the light of the sun, of the moon, and of the stars into the rooms, not only through a few windows, but through as many walls as feasible, these to consist entirely of glass-coloured glass.'

The Glass Pavilion was more than an exhibition building; it was conceived to exploit an alternative technical virtuosity. The octagonal form was comprised of a crystalline faceted dome, defined by its concrete skeleton, all inlaid with coloured glass plates that acted like mirrors on the façade. Within the faceted interior, angled outer plates restricted external views and filtered the daylight into a soft spatial luminosity. The building was designed as an essay in coloured beauty, 'a little temple of beauty', and Taut described the 'reflections of light' in the pavilion, 'whose colours began at the base with a dark blue and rose up through moss green and golden yellow to culminate at the top in a luminous pale yellow.' These reflections were orchestrated by bright, internal lighting features. The impact of Scheerbart's philosophy was made manifest by Taut in his Glass Pavilion.

This concept changed the perception of space in architecture because it combined the inherent material characteristics of glass with light, transparency, reflection, translucency and opacity. At the same time Mies van der Rohe, who was sympathetic to the expressionist ideals reflected in glass architecture, sought to develop a building 'evolving from the inside', combining glass with the advantages of the new steel-framed structures. In his concepts for skyscrapers in Berlin in 1921/22 he explored the idea of constructing the wall of a building entirely of glass. Glass as a 'skin' would be slipped over the steel structure, and the building's 'skin and bones' would allow the glass to mirror, reflect and integrate with the structure, rather than conceal it. As he so prophetically stated: 'The use of glass does compel us to go new ways.'

Mies's ideas for spatiality were subsequently explored in the Tugendhat House and the Barcelona Pavilion. Both derived their plan from free-flowing space, divided by inner walls as horizontal planes, using the outer glass envelope as a means to eliminate the visual interruption between inside and outside, and to frame the views. The walls were not entirely glass, but were designed with glass as an essential component. They were transparent at some points and translucent at others, and were made of large full-height, floor-to-ceiling panes. Meanwhile, Frank Lloyd Wright in the United States was also pursuing the notion of opening up space, 'destroying the box', dissolving the division between interior and exterior. He was to 'consider glass as the most precious of materials to generate a new relationship between mankind and nature. Glass and light – two forms of the same thing!'

Also in this same period, Le Corbusier in Paris was postulating other possibilities for an open architecture that provided for light, air and sunshine through poetic fluid space and the further development of the wall and the use of glass. His idea for long windows, or *pan de verre*, was extolled in his design for the Villa Savoye (1931). Also, in his Cité de Refuge (1930–33), by recognizing the associated issue of climatic control, Le Corbusier was the first to attempt (though it was to fail) an integrated curtain wall system. It was to take the glass industry a further 50 years to reconcile the environmental challenges of the curtain wall, and control the impact of solar gain by tinting, air-conditioning, integral multilayered façades and various shading devices.

Meanwhile, the success of Chareau's Maison de Verre (*see above*) was to have the more influence on the use of glass (Le Corbusier visited the house a number of times during its construction). Whereas Le Corbusier's

buildings were about the active interplay of solids and voids, Chareau's house was about translucency and light modifying form through a skeletal structure and a glass envelope – an envelope that captured, filtered and transformed the space through light, both during the day and at night.

Within the house this concept was further developed by the use of mobile screens, which were perforated and sliding. These internal screens were used as a 'veil', to both consciously and unconsciously explore the ideas of viewing, observing, and being anti-voyeuristic, while theatrically interpreting the duality of show and display. This was developed as a profound response to the ideas of gazing and space.

Dematerialization: Luminosity and sublime space
It is notable that after the radicalism of the 1930s in Europe, and the philosophic proclamations of a 'new era of glass', for the next 50 years the wider potential of glass was comprehensively redirected by a singular focus: that of the curtain wall and its resultant technology. Although glass was universally adopted as the symbol of progress and mass commercialization, particularly in the United States as a sign of prosperity, its application as a material with specific properties was largely overlooked. The opportunities for utilizing glass as a richer substance with significant material qualities were devalued and it was seen as a superficial cladding material, its surface qualities providing the minimal envelope. As a result its proliferation was defined by its role as the corporate image-builder of modern architecture.

Between the pioneering influences of Taut and Chareau, and the chief protagonists Le Corbusier and Mies van der Rohe, glass was mainly associated with the technological specialization of the façade and environmental functions. The preoccupation with the façade was initially a necessity to allow for the continuity of space and to facilitate a new architecture of transparency and openness, making use of opportunities from industry and new technology. Flexibility and comfort, liberation of light and space, were realized through the free plan (achieved by separating the loadbearing elements) and façade (which permitted large horizontal window openings in the plane of the elevations).

The radicality of Le Corbusier's Villa Savoye was a result of the fluidity of the three-dimensional spaces. Mies's concentration on steel and glass, on the other hand, moved the focus away from the structure of space towards the building envelope by utilizing full-height plate glass between steel stanchions, which created a highly articulated effect though a minimalistic and formalistic language. This was most vividly postulated in his Farnsworth House, a single-glazed villa in Illinois (1946) (*see page 18*). Large horizontal expanses of glass set within a raised steel structure, all in an untouched landscape of trees by a river, provided an idealized setting that echoed Japanese sensibilities about nature and space. It became an icon of modern architecture and persisted as a monumental metaphor for the architecture of transparency and reflection. And in so doing it delayed the onset of a true emergence of glass architecture.

Following Mies's transparent container, architects of the 1970s and 1980s, such as Norman Foster, Richard Rogers and Rice Francis Ritchie, sought to perfect and develop the heritage of Farnsworth House, helped by the glass industry. While the industry developed various new sealant methods – using rubber, neoprene and silicone – architects successfully developed new glass-supporting systems such as suspended glazing, patch fittings, planar systems, point fixings with tension cables, glazed nets and cable lattice façades, and experimented with load bearing glass walls.

While these technological advances did much to raise awareness of building in glass, they were essentially reinterpretations of the minimal glass box. They were essays in lightness of construction, rather than construction with light where the aesthetic use of glass is based on a more profound awareness of what transparency can mean to architecture's own specificity.

Gyorgy Kepes wrote in 1944: 'Transparency implies more than one optical characteristic, it implies a broader spatial order. Transparency means a simultaneous perception of different spatial locations. Space not only recedes but fluctuates in a continuous activity. The position of the transparent figures has a equivocal meaning as one sees each figure now as the closer, now as the further.' The notion that transparency is remote from that which is perfectly clear, is in fact close to the notion that it is clearly ambiguous. The distinction is between the real or 'literal transparency' and a 'phenomenal transparency', or seeming to be transparent. There is a characteristic of transparency

that provides a constant dialogue between fact and implication. One senses the materiality of space through the plane dividing an inner and outer world. Understanding the materiality of space through light is central to this synthesis of functions. Space is constructed, and is made substantial, through its own tangibility. In the use of glass in architecture the phenomenology of transparency provides the opportunity to transform space by crystallizing its translucence, linking our sense of dematerialization and our articulation of perceptual experiences.

Ironically, it was not architects who made the key transformation in the phenomenology of glass, but artists. In the mid-1960s, a small group of 'light artists' were experimenting in southern California with the notion of art/objects, without the presence of the object – experimenting with light and dark, sunlight and shadow, time and space, sound and silence, using mixed materials such as Plexiglas, polyester resin, cast acrylic, fibreglass, dielectricoated glass, and luminescent and phosphorescent agents. They were not a defined movement, rather artists all working in the fields of the experiential, situational, phenomenal, and site-specific, simply using light and space.

The key artists of that period were Robert Irwin, James Turrell, Doug Wheeler, Larry Bell and Eric Orr. They worked mainly by trial and error adopting a philosophical stance, 'examining your existence in the world … a kind of primal intuition'. They drew their frame of reference from the Russian Suprematists of 1915 and the Realists of the 1920s. The Suprematists work, such as that of Kasimir Malevich and El Lissitzky,

proclaimed 'metaphysical implications for art, an art without objects'. Whereas the Suprematists sought to evoke abstract art, Realists such as Ivan Kudrjaschow pursued architectonic sensations, with new perceptions of colour and light in works called *Luminescence*. As Ivan Klyun wrote in 1925: 'Material existence can only be apprehended through perception. Ideas and thoughts are in essence products of material processes.'

The light and space artists were also inspired by the literal use of light, referred to as 'Luminism', which combined art and the technology of light production. Transparency and immateriality were a key focus, with a number of major artists in southern California utilizing glass and plastic to combine light, space and colour in order to dissolve the boundary between art and sculpture. Also media-based artists explored opacity, the translucence of plastic, opalescent colour and engineered art pieces.

At the same time the work of West Coast artists pursuing minimalism, such as Donald Judd, Dan Flavin, Dan Graham and Robert Morris, also had an influence. Reducing 'art to an essence in pure realism' through the use of industrial materials, such as steel, aluminium, fluorescent light, mirrors and sheet glass, to express particular phenomena, they created illusions on water, and projected and reflected light. However, much of the light and space work did not receive critical acclaim in the United States at the time. Among the exceptions were Robert Irwin's *Filigree /Line/Plane* at Wellesley (1980) and *9 Spaces, 9 Trees* (1979–83) at Seattle, and James Turrell's *Rondo* light installation at the Newport

Harbor Art Museum (1969) and his *Wedgewood III* light installation at the Whitney Museum New York (1980–81).

It was decades before the key link between the work of these artists in the 1960s and the emergent glass architects fully crossed boundaries and made an impact. Crucially, it was James Turrell, who trained first as a psychologist and then as a light artist, who made the perceptual bridge – to 'take light and make it material'.

Architecturally, the first building to explore the promise of a new transparency was the Willis Faber & Dumas offices in Ipswich, England (1971–75), by Foster Associates (Norman Foster) (*see above*). This project features an undulating glass curtain-wall, visually recapturing the work of Robert Morris which had considered the fine line between sculpture and architecture. The elevations were conceived of as entirely 'seamless', although made up of glass panels fixed at corners by patch fittings, and braced from within the interior by half-storey-height glass fins. The glass is butt-jointed, and uses silicone joints to maintain visual continuity and provide an even-weather seal.

The curved façade, which simply follows the site's shape, uses Pilkington single-glazed toughened solar-tinted glass. This provides body to the surface and causes a dramatic shimmering effect, resulting in multiple reflections of the surrounding streetscape, while the interior produces reflections between inside and out. At night the lighting levels within the building cause an inversion of the day effect, bringing the

Far left The glass façade of Mies van der Rohe's Farnsworth House in Illinois (1946). The building became an icon for modern architecture and persisted as a metaphor for the architecture of reflection and transparency.

Left Foster Associates' offices for Willis Faber & Dumas (1971–75). It was the first building to explore the promise of a new transparency in glass architecture.

building to life as a true architecture of transparency and so dematerializing the spatial boundaries.

Alchemy: To the lightness of being

'What used to be the boundary of material, its terminus, has become an entryway hidden in the most imperceptible entity. From here on, the appearance of surfaces and superficies conceals a secret transparency, a thickness without thickness, a volume without volume, an imperceptible quantity.'
Marc Taylor-Hidden

The 1990s represents an epoch quite different from earlier periods of technological change. In this period the wider availability of glass, the greater choice of materials and material finishes, the ability to resolve climatic considerations technologically and, above all, an aesthetic – a desire for transparency, space and light – all had a culminative effect on the opportunities architects had to experiment with glass architecture and demonstrate glass technology in buildings.

Following numerous developments by the glass industry during the 1980s – the evolution of hard and soft coatings on the inner surface of the glass envelope, double and triple skins, solar-control glasses, K-insulation glass, integral blind and shading devices, and thinner composite constructions – the multiple envelope could begin to accommodate integral climatic control (thermal regulation and energy recovery) and realize the goal of a pure façade. Through these technological advances the real potential for dematerialization of space and an allusive architecture could be emphasized. Due to the focus of technological specialization, the façade could be realized as a series of separate layers, each one having a key function within the multiplicity of the interlayers, and each one collectively merging within the façade's overall effect. Embedded in this investigation were new possibilities of lightness, evanescent spaces, superimposition, ephemeral registration of depth of surface and an autonomy of the surface skin.

This becomes an impressive theme in Peter Zumthor's Kunsthaus in Austria (1991) (*see pages 24–31*). The building is a monolithic cube that consists of two primary materials: polished concrete and opaque glass. The main structure and the elements consist of a concrete building, all wrapped by regular elevations of etched glass that are configured as a 'scaly' external skin, around a solid sculptural core. One is clearly a foil to the other. The glass is both a veil to the interior and stunning shell that provides a lantern of light, a visualization of the invisible material of glass. The net effect is a building that has a magnetic chemistry – it appears dull and opaque against the sky on grey days, and when the sun shines the surface is enlivened, the glow rendering its density and materiality clearly visible. This dual alchemy varies between transparency and translucency, and the hyperreality of the allure of what is behind and what is within.

Similarly, with Herzog & de Meuron's Goetz Collection in Munich (1994) (*see pages 48–54*) – a detached building in a parkland setting – the building consists of two wrapped opaque bands of green glass, one at the top and the other at the bottom, with a wider band of birchwood cladding panels in the middle. The building's presence on the site changes from a two-dimensional plane to a floating transparent volume that embodies sensuality and lightness of being. Apart from being a thermal and acoustic insulator, the double glass is a kind of veil that announces, without revealing, the reverse side of the façade. This type of uniform – a dense and smooth skin – advocates minimalist techniques. The architectural mass is concealed from the surrounding context and this helps to reduce the building's impact, reducing the connection between the interior and exterior and undermining the weight of matter through translucency.

In Jean Nouvel's Arab Institute in Paris (1987) (*see page 20*), the main southern façades are a mechanical response to this layering effect, consisting entirely of camera shutters that create superimpositions and reflections, and act like a photographic plate of the Parisian cityscape, while the elevations manipulate the treatment of light into the dark interior by means of frames and filters in deep shadows. Photosensitive motorized diaphragms trigger the change of light, and the interior translates sudden changes of light levels, spatial volumes and sensations of openness and closure. The building becomes a surface that acts as a screen to, and between, the world within and the surroundings. Jean Nouvel interprets his façades as 'mirror images of our world overflowing with information', but also as sensationalized embellishments of surface.

In his later project, the Fondation Cartier (1991-94) (*see pages 56–64*), the multiplicity of the façades' interlayers is exploited to even greater effect without recourse to

mechanical devices or obvious technological means. The building represents a visual 'paradox of the immateriality of nature and the inexorable materiality of architecture'. The building borrows from the metaphor of cinema. Creating a series of frames and screening devices that seem to sequence and distil phases from a scene, its gridded narrative creates an *auteur* quality. As a consequence there are various readings of the building's synthesis. One hypothesis is that both cinema and architecture depend on light. In the words of Jean Nouvel: 'Light is matter, and light is a basic material. Once you understand how light varies, and varies our perceptions, your architectural vocabulary is immediately extended, in ways that classical architecture never thought of …. An architecture of ephemerality becomes possible.'

It is this quality that gives the building its presence – it is both ambiguous and complex, and this provides a tension and edge to the whole that is essentially evanescent in character. It is also reminiscent of the earlier works of Californian media/light artists such as Laddie John Dill and minimalists such as Dan Graham whose works experimented with solid forms dissolving through reflected or projected light. Images were superimposed between the interplay of light coming from the surroundings and light coming from the inner spaces.

Similarly, Design Antenna's glass pavilion at Broadfield House in England (1994) (*see pages 66–73*) captures the immateriality and virtuality of presence in the building. From the exterior the architecture is exposed, naked and evanescent – a homage to the minimal

Miesian glass volume, a complete essay on all-glass construction techniques – but from within the exterior context the surroundings and sky are revealed as a super-realistic ambiguity, where the boundaries of the architecture are charged with a sensorial sense of spatiality and a quality of lightness. This expression of the *floue* (blurred) image – an elimination of borders of materiality – is distilled by the use of banded frit-patterning on the roof, which with the silver soft coating on the glass, plays with the depth of field and intentionally seeks to mystify the normal sense of dimensionality.

The Balearic Technological and European Business Innovation Centre in Majorca by Alberto Campo Baeza (1998) (*see pages 98–107*) takes these preoccupations into a poetic translation of gravity and light through physical reality by the use of lightweight tectonic elements of stone and glass that are transformed by light. According to the architect: 'Gravity constructs space; light constructs time, makes time meaningful. The central concerns of architecture are how to control gravity and how to relate to light. Indeed, the very future of architecture depends on whether a new understanding of these phenomena can be achieved.'

In Ibos and Vitart's Museum of Art in France (1997) (*see pages 74–81*), the experiential qualities of ambiguity are taken a stage further. A new, blade-like extension offers a seamless fully glazed façade adjacent to the original Beaux Arts building. It both reflects the context on its surface and, within the depth of the all-glass elevation, generates a pixelated mirage of ephemeral registrations

that provides an almost cinematic animation of the scene and an enigmatic architectural resolution.

The 'determination of existential space' places the architect as the translator, interpreter or choreographer of the immaterial qualities of contemporary illusory architecture. Creating the façade is no longer just designing the elevation; it has its own reality of surface and an implied depth of virtual dimensionality. Symbolic functions have been largely lost to artistic responses that resist the architecture being a resolution of structure, support and environmental climatic control. Modern building techniques largely conceal the true intent of the façade, and have transformed the appearance of the otherwise unitary envelope.

Glass and translucent materials do not necessarily open up the architecture to reveal space. Instead they adopt an ambiguous stance and demonstrate the autonomy of the cladding to the whole. With the increasing focus on surface, the nature of the material becomes the key focus of the architectural enquiry; and the materiality the basis for conceptualizing the desired appearance of the material, its aesthetic and tactile qualities, its colour, texture and sensorial characteristics.

For Herzog & de Meuron the exploration of surface is still one of the principal themes of their architecture, within which they view architecture 'as an act of communication, not represented by fixed forms but by an oscillating field of perception' (Xavier Gonzalez). They achieve this by redefining the relationship of surface to volume, and by dissolving the façades into immaterial pictorial layers. This approach is as much a reference to 'skin' as an epidermal concept as it is to it as a layer that envelops space. For various architects exploring this dialogue it is a duality between the autonomy of the epidermis and the pre-eminence of the material, in this case glass.

This is used to conceal both the composition of the traditional façade and the substance of the solid form; but also, variously, it utilizes the technological potential of the wrappings, and exploits the camouflage as an outer cover or undefined coating. In Rafael Moneo's Kursaal Centre in Spain (1999) (see pages 116–125), the architect turns two cuboid forms into luminous boxes by the use of layers of concave glass profiles that conceal the public function within.

Similarly, in Erick van Egeraat's later building, the city hall in the Alphen aan den Rijn in the Netherlands (2002) (see pages 184–191), the wrapping becomes a complete tattooed envelope. Leaf patterns are fritted on to the glass surface by means of a series of stencil-like multiple imprints. The effect on the glass helps to regulate daylight and moderate heat, while internally the spatial effect is one of walking through a shadowy forest. This technique has been exploited by other architects, including Norman Foster (Stockley Park, 1989), Jean Nouvel (DuMont Schauberg and Media Park, Cologne, 1990–91), Toyo Ito (Sendai Médiathèque, 2001), Francis Soler (private apartments in Paris, 1997), Günter Behnisch (Bad Elster Swimming Pool, 1999), Markus Allmann (Neuhausen Church, 2000), Will Alsop (Colorium, 2001) and Herzog & de Meuron (Laban Dance Centre, 2003).

For Herzog & de Meuron the material is the 'medium upon which the message is written', and in the case of Jean Nouvel it transforms the façade into a projection screen. Similarly, in Toyo Ito's Tower of the Winds in Yokohama (1995), electronic light mutates the imagery of the glass architecture. Just as Gothic stained-glass windows communicated religious information by means of natural light, so the contemporary façade has become a media screen, integrating the latest information technology.

However, the way in which glass architecture since 2000 has begun to engage beyond the surface has been altogether more seamless. Rather than exploiting the art of technology at the surface as a means of technical prowess, there is a growing discourse of iteration in articulating light, manipulating surface and exploring volume. Through this informed wisdom about the applications of glass, as both medium and material, there is a more profound understanding of space that is intelligent, poetically precise and visually magnificent. This wisdom has multiplicity, and yet has a singular condensed concept – that of glass as medium, as a revelation for light and matter.

Part of this informed approach can be perceived in the body of architectural work by Steven Holl. He puts it thus: 'Perception and cognition balance the volumetrics of architectural spaces with the understanding of time itself. An ecstatic architecture of the immeasurable emerges. It is precisely at this level of spatial perception that the most powerful architectural meanings come to the fore.'

Holl has systematically explored the differing optical conditions in relation to space, in order to explore new perspectives and perceptions with light. This enquiry originated with his offices for D.E. Shaw in New York (1992) (see pages 32–39), and was later extended in his Kiasma Museum of Contemporary Art in Finland (1993) (see pages 40–47), and his Chapel of Ignatius in the United States (1997) (see pages 82–89). The museum was particularly inspired by sequential experiences of space in parallax which, combined with luminous flux, played with personal perceptions. He exploits edges, contours and surfaces to reveal dynamic perception through light, either as the chiaroscuro of projected shadows or gauze-like ribbons of prismatic night effects. Holl's revelations of new spaces have a recurring theme of dissolving and reappearing with light; light that changes and appears to describe form; light that is not only seen with eyes but is felt, and which imbues an architecture with a 'lightness of being'. This lightness is about constructing with light through glass.

The path of any creative encounter entails the abstract and the concrete. In architecture this journey must lead the conceptual and the abstract towards formulation. In the case of glass, this odyssey is ongoing in its search for meaning. For glass architecture the search for a 'lightness of being' is perhaps a timeless reality. One that has undergone a significant metamorphosis, but which continues its transformation from the physical to the sensorial and which in its poetic state is at once transient, transcendental and profound. But above all it is arousing and inspiring. And so the journey continues … towards the light.

Case studies

Left Concept sketch – the building was conceived as a 'museum of daylight', with no deviations at all in the glass panels that cover the entire exterior surface.

Opposite One side of the building defines a square that links the Kunsthaus to the city beyond.

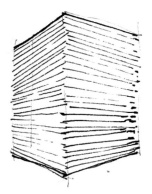

Kunsthaus Bregenz, Austria 1991

Architects
Atelier Peter Zumthor

Client
Land Voralberg

Programme
Art galleries
Lecture room
Educational centre
Maintenance facilities
Archive
Workshops
Library
Café
Museum shop

Location
The Kunsthaus Bregenz sits in a prominent location not far from the eastern end of Lake Constance – a popular tourist destination in northern Austria. It fills the space on Seestrasse between the Vorarlberg Theatre and the main post office which has stood empty for many years. The entrance lies on the eastern side of the building facing the town. The administration building, situated in front of the museum towards the city centre, acts as a transitional structure relating to the smaller buildings of the old town. All the functional facilities of the Kunsthaus, other than those directly associated with the presentation of art, are housed separately in this smaller building, which accommodates a library, the museum shop and a café as well as the administrative offices.

Site Description
The exhibition building and the administration building frame an open square, which is closed off on the south by the back wall of the adjacent theatre. On one side, however, the site opens up towards the city to create a square that links the Kunsthaus to the city. The square is used by the museum for open-air art events and is occupied by the museum café during the warmer months, encouraging the diversity of city life down towards the lakefront.

Building Solution
The Kunsthaus Bregenz, a mysterious translucent monolith, was conceived as a 'museum of daylight'. With only the minimum necessary openings at ground level and no deviations at all in the glass panels that cover the rest of the building's exterior surface, the only transgressions are the traces of human forms moving behind the taut glass walls. Described by the architect as looking like 'slightly ruffled feathers or like a scaly structure', the façade is comprised of 712 glass shingles, measuring 1.7 by 2.9 metres (5.5 by 9.5 feet) each, serving as a skin to diffuse daylight throughout the building.

The façade is designed as a self-supporting structure, completely independent of the concrete structural shell of the building proper. A steel framework supports the glass shingles on the exterior as well as an inner layer of glass to create a double-layered sheath that covers the free-standing concrete building within. Between the outer and inner layers of glass, a 90 centimetre (35 inch) wide light pit makes it possible to direct daylight to the first subterranean level as well as accommodating the lighting installation that illuminates the Kunsthaus by night. Resting on metal brackets and held in place by large clamps, the edges of the glass are exposed so that air and light can penetrate through the open joints of the outer surface.

The galleries themselves are at the centre of the organizational strategy of the building, arranged within a simple rectangular prism. Below the galleries are two levels of subterranean support facilities including a lecture room, educational centre, maintenance rooms, archive, workshops and plant facilities. Above these, the ground floor accommodates the entrance foyer, and ticket desk. The three upper floors containing the galleries have ceilings of square glass panels etched on the underside and linked by chrome connectors which themselves are hung from the underside of the slab above.

Slab and ceiling are over 2 metres (6.5 feet) apart so above every ceiling is a void that acts as a plenum for both air and light. Diffused light pours in through the frosted-skin of the building and down via the frosted-glass ceiling where it is supplemented by automatically controlled artificial lighting at the centre

Below A staircase running almost the full width of one glass façade links all the galleries above ground level.

Opposite Daylight is supplemented by specially designed pendant fittings that are controlled by an exterior sensor. Each light can be modulated individually or as part of a group to create specific light levels for individual works of art, or for an exhibition.

and the perimeter. Consisting of specially developed pendulum lamps, controlled by an exterior light sensor on the roof, each light can be controlled separately or as part of a group to create the specific light levels required for each exhibition, or for individual works within an exhibition.

The extraordinary effect is that each gallery feels as if it is day-lit directly from above, with only the flimsiest of filtering devices between the viewer and the sky. Although the light has been refracted three times (through the glass façade, the insulating inner layer of glass and the glass ceilings), it illuminates the galleries differently depending on the time of day or year so that one is always aware of external conditions. In this way, an atmosphere of natural lighting is created despite the fact that the building has no windows, or at least none in the conventional sense.

Below Detail view of the glass shingles that make up the outer layer of a double sheath of glass covering the building.

Opposite The glass shingles, resting on metal brackets and held in place by large clamps, are arranged so that light and air can penetrate through the open joints of the outer surface.

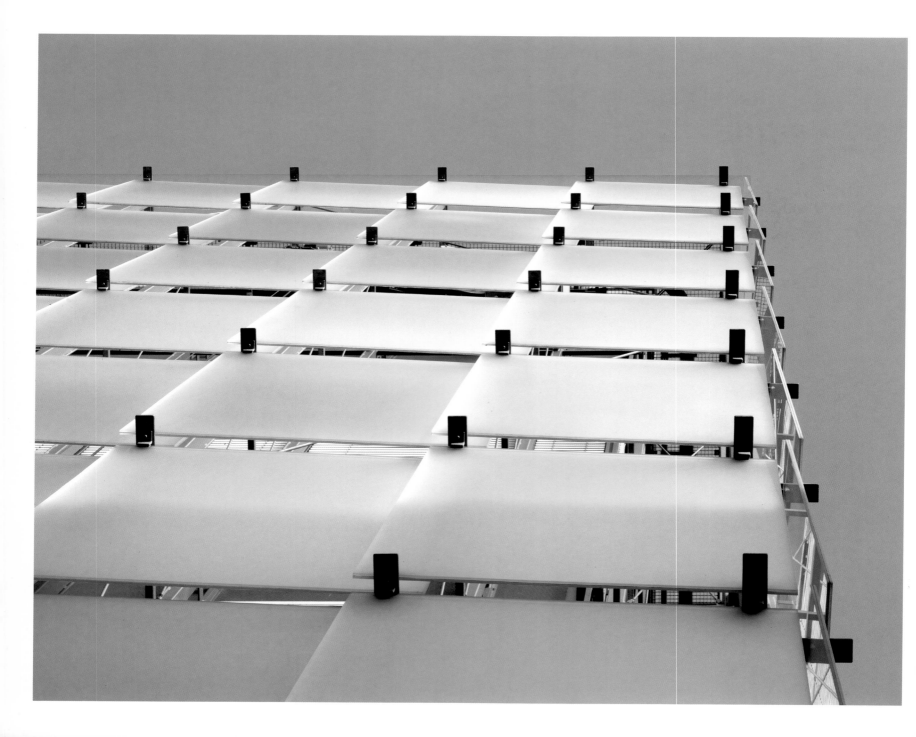

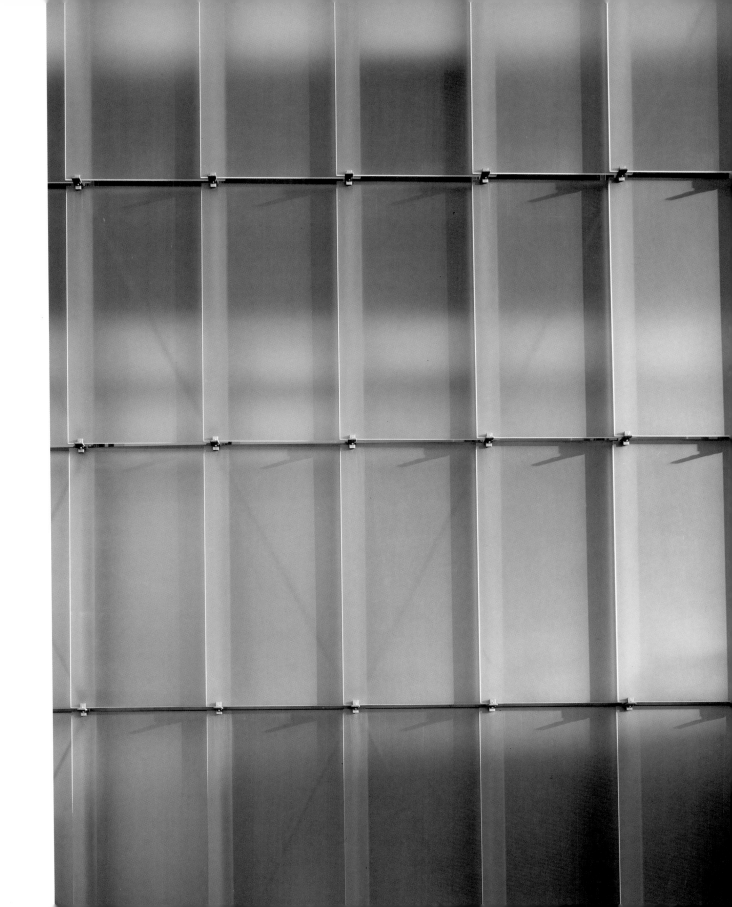

Opposite At night soft light pours from the glass surface, turning the building into an urban icon.

Below Floor plans and sections – the building houses two basement levels of galleries (as well as support facilities), three upper gallery levels, and the ground-floor entrance and ticket office.

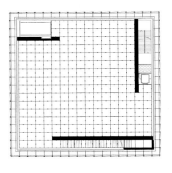

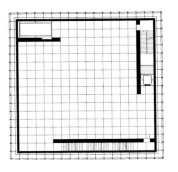

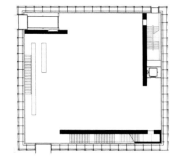

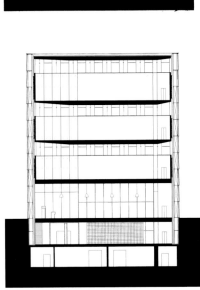

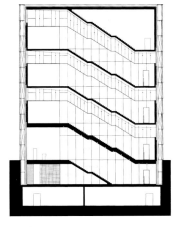

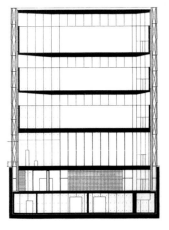

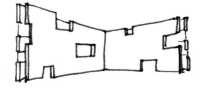

Shaw Offices
New York, USA
1992

Architects
Steven Holl Architects

Client
D. E. Shaw & Co.

Programme
Office and trading area

Location

Located in the top two floors of a 40-storey tower in midtown Manhattan, D.E. Shaw & Co, founded in 1988 by David Shaw, a former professor of computer science, consider themselves to be mavericks in the financial world. The company's 65-person team uses some 300 computers to execute transactions 22.5 hours a day, resting only between the time that the Tokyo exchange closes and London opens. To generate profits on decimal-point price shifts, Shaw has assembled a staff consisting mostly of computer scientists and mathematicians, who devise strategies for four to six full-time traders. In recognition of his organization's unusual occupation, Shaw required a working environment that was unlike a typical corporate Wall Street office, and that would reflect the team's non-conformist attitude to its work.

Site Description

The brief required that the 1,022 square metre (11,000 square foot) space be designed and built in minimal time (just six months from the date of commission to moving in), and on a spartan budget. Using the site provided – two levels of rather conventional commercial office space – and the unusual nature of the client as the point of departure, Holl hoped to capture something of the ephemeral nature of trading that relies on memory chips and satellites. Recognizing that his favoured palette of materials, including tinted plaster, cast glass and terrazzo would not be possible in this project, Holl planned to design the space using little more than space and light, which he describes as 'the only free materials'.

Building Solution

The programme for D.E. Shaw is straightforward: a series of private offices and semi-private workstations, a conference room and a compact trading room. There was no requirement for a public space or a means of displaying the company's prosperity, since as a proprietary trader the company's only client is itself. A singular and spectacular statement is made, however, through the insertion of a double-height space at the heart of the scheme, used as both a reception area and a social gathering space, as well as the departure point for a number of spatial sequences that gradually unfold towards the exterior of the building. In contrast to the monitors and other technical equipment piled high on the workstations, this space, measuring 6.5 metres wide by 8.5 metres long by 9 metres high (21 by 28 by 30 feet), is a supremely serene environment, inspiring quiet contemplation rather than the frenetic monitoring of the international marketplace.

The central concept for the design is derived from the company's total reliance on computers and telecommunications, what Holl refers to as 'the invisible technology of electricity'. Harnessing this invisible source of light, the experimental design explores the phenomena of spatial colour reflection or 'projected colour'. The reception space is surrounded by a thick wall of metal-framed plasterboard that is carved and notched at precise points. These notches, lit by coloured artificial light by night and reflected sunlight by day, evoke electricity in the form of energy pulsating between the two layers of the walls. Colour has been applied to the back or bottom surfaces of the cut-outs, which are invisible to the viewer within the space. The natural and artificial light projects this colour back into the space around the walls and fissures. The overall luminescence within the building is intensified by the sheen of the waxed black vinyl floor, giving the space an unexpected extra dimension that goes beyond the six sides of the cube.

Despite the fact that the reception area's layered north wall mostly blocks vistas of Manhattan's spectacular skyline, small glass side panels tightly crop portions of adjacent towers, bringing the gridded façades into sharp focus and rendering them as, appropriately, something akin to a computer chip. Glass is employed at D. E. Shaw not as a material to be treasured or admired in its own right, for its crystalline properties. Rather, the views and light that the space came with have been almost entirely blocked out by solid walls. Views and light are then reintroduced through the careful placement of small but precise glass elements, to provide a carefully crafted spatial environment. Light, transmitted and refracted and reflected through glass and over painted surfaces, creates a calming glow that changes in mood by day and by night as one moves around, into and out of this ephemeral space.

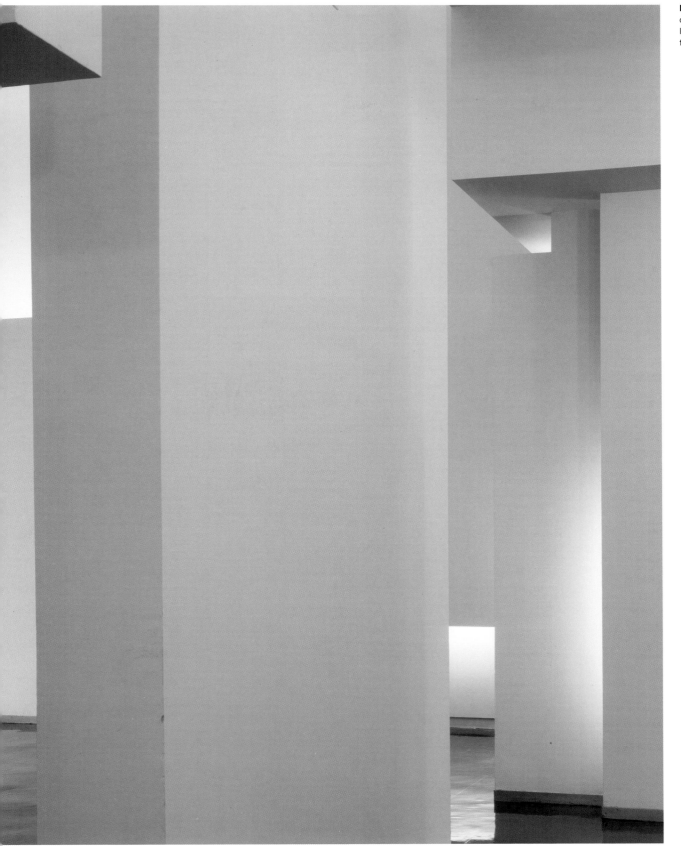

Left During the day, daylight reflects off the coloured surfaces concealed within the notches, lending an unexpectedly serene atmosphere to the offices.

Below Detail view of the upper level of the tinted plaster wall.

Opposite View of the reception area.

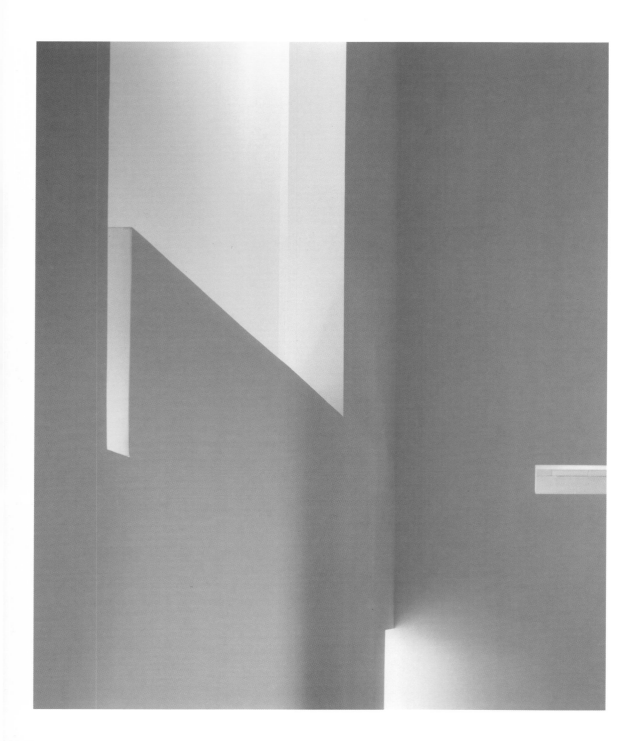

Opposite While the wall conceals views of Manhattan's spectacular skyline, small areas of clear glazing crop vistas of adjacent towers.

Below Axonometric view showing the arrangement of the notched wall; floor plan.

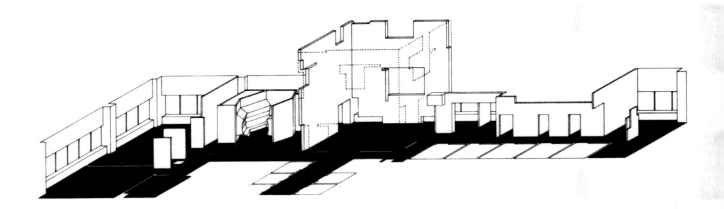

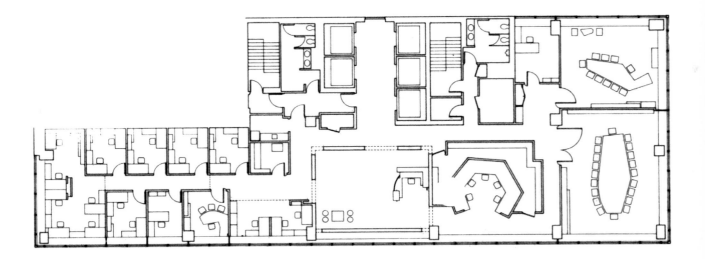

Kiasma Museum of Contemporary Art Helsinki, Finland 1993

Architects
Steven Holl Architects

Client
Finnish Ministry of Education /
Museum of Contemporary Art,
Finnish National Gallery

Programme
Art galleries
Museum shop
Café
Workshops
Storage facilities

Location

Kiasma, the Museum of Contemporary Art, lies in the heart of Helsinki at the foot of the parliament building to the west, with Eliel Saarinen's Helsinki station to the west, and Alvar Aalto's Finlandia Hall to the north. The challenging nature of the site stems from the proximity of these monuments of modern architecture, the confluence of the various city grids, and from the triangular shape of the site that nonetheless has the potential to open up towards the natural landscape of Töölö Bay in the distance.

Site Description

The concept of Kiasma involves intertwining the building mass with the geometry of the city and the landscape, which are reflected in the form of the building. An implicit cultural line curves to link the building to Finlandia Hall, while also engaging a topographic line connecting to the wider landscape and Töölö Bay. The masterplan for the area which had been put forward by Alvar Aalto in the 1960s, includes the extension of the bay right up to the museum to create an area for future civic development along the southern foreshore as well as serving as a reflection pool for Finlandia Hall.

Building Solution

Chiasma, derived from the Greek letter chi and meaning a crossing or exchange, was the code word used by Steven Holl to identify his entry for the 1993 design competition for the new national museum of contemporary art. For Holl, the word encapsulated the conceptual underpinning of the scheme, which he describes as, 'the joining of interior mystery with exterior horizon [like] two hands clasping'. The adoption of the Finnish translation, *kiasma*, as the permanent name for the building underlines the aptness of the concept and Holl's perceptive interpretation of the brief.

The scheme comprises three elements: a bar of water and two bars of building. By pushing the building right to the east of the site, a new reflecting pool is defined. The western building is orthogonal, while the eastern bar, a twisted curvilinear form, is sheared off on its south and east façades as it comes into contact with the city grid. At the north end of the site, the three bars intersect and the open end of the curved form becomes the dominant feature reaching out to the landscape. The north elevation records the many geometries exerting an influence on the site. Here the water crosses through the building

and falls to a small pool, indicating the connection between the reflecting pool and the extension of Töölö Bay.

Back-of-house facilities such as vehicle access for parking and deliveries, workshops, storage and mechanical plant are tucked away at lower ground level so that the upper ground level can be given over entirely to public facilities. Staff offices, cloakrooms and an auditorium are located on the east side of the building, while to the west are the ticket desk, the shop and café which opens out onto a terrace and the reflecting pool. The main entrance is approached across a granite-paved courtyard where a steel-framed glazed canopy extends outwards from the vertical fissure between the two buildings, drawing visitors towards it.

Inside, a slender, elongated warped void defines the heart of the museum. Here, a ramp climbs up the curved east wall to arrive at the critical crossing point of building and water. The first level of galleries is reached from this landing, while suites of double-height galleries step up the building in four split levels on alternate sides of the central void. The underlying order of the building, however, is not in the arrangement of the galleries, but in the circulation and the

manipulation of natural light. There is no one privileged or prescribed route through the building. Multiple lifts, stairs and ramps combine with the split-level galleries to create many possible itineraries. The routes between rooms are on the diagonal, in a zigzag trajectory, or within a double-height top-lit aisle against the curved north-eastern façade, but always returning to the central void.

The circulation, in its turn, is tied to the curved geometry which is designed to capture the elusive horizontal light in this northern latitude. Shaped in plan to mirror the arc of the winter sun, the wall also rotates from a 9.5 degree outward tilt at its southern end to a 9.5 degree inward tilt at the northern end. The galleries themselves are also attuned to the quality and origin of natural light. The lower galleries have flat ceilings and receive daylight through the translucent glass curtain wall. Moving up through the building, the ceilings become more sculptural, and deep shafts carved into the curved profile at the north-east end bring light unexpectedly into the middle-level galleries. The uppermost gallery is a dramatically top-lit vaulted space.

Much of the daylight in the building is diffused by translucent glass which intensifies the weak northern light and lends a sense of contemplative detachment from the life of the city. Release is provided in the form of clear glazing at significant points in the building. Even in these instances, the experience and the light are controlled. For example, the slender vertical slice of city viewed from the south façade contrasts markedly with the sweeping panorama offered by the expanse of clear glazing in the north façade. On the eastern façade, a small crescent window reveals a glimpse of the railway station and marks the juncture between the orthogonal and the curvilinear forms.

With the galleries in operation 12 hours a day, natural light cannot be relied upon at this northern latitude; indeed, during the winter there are several months of darkness. As a result, each gallery has two sources of artificial light – fluorescents concealed by light shelves and flexible, ceiling-mounted spotlights. The multiple configurations of warm artificial light and cool natural light enrich the experience of the spaces, which is enhanced by the subtly judged palette of finishes. The roughly plastered white-painted walls and black concrete floors throw off shades of watercolour grey, in an abstract and painterly composition. Glass and natural light are also used to great effect on the exterior. The double-curved east wall of the void is expressed externally as a wall of translucent glass planks. Vertical surfaces are sheathed with a rain screen of aluminium panels combined with glazed curtain walling, while the curved north-east end of the building is clad with prepatinated zinc. On a cloudy day the building takes on the leaden hue of the sky, but with the appearance of the sun the glass, aluminium and zinc glow with reflected light. At night, the polarity of light is reversed. Lit from within, the museum becomes a lantern of shades of white created by the combinations of clear and translucent glazing. This quiet essay in the juxtaposition of light and dark, white and black, line and curve is a finely judged, even celebratory mono-chromatic rendering of light, in answer to the Arctic peculiarities of the Finnish culture, climate and light.

Top View of the entrance which is approached via a granite-paved courtyard.

Centre The northern end of the building is almost entirely glazed to make a connection with the landscape. The multiple geometries inscribed on its surface record the many factors that exert an influence on the site.

Bottom Detail view of the copper-clad roof, in which small sections apparently peel back, creating additional opportunities for daylight to penetrate the interior.

5 Viides kerros Femte våningen Fifth floor
Yinka Shonibare
Lainahöyhenissä
Dubbel dräkt
Double Dress 25.1.–1.6.

4 4
Yinka Shonibare
Lainahöyhenissä
Dubbel dräkt
Double Dress 25.1.–1.6.

Kontti
DEMOSKENE.KATASTRO.FI
28 3.–15.6.2003

3 3
yöjuna
nattåget
night train
15.3.2003–29.2.2004
Kokoelmat Samlingarna Collections

Huone X Rum X Room X

2 Printti
yöjuna
nattåget
night train
15.3.2003–29.2.2004
Kokoelmat Samlingarna Collections

Studio K
Tarja Pitkänen-Walter
"Maalaus on lihan kiilto silm
14.2.–18.5.2003

Opposite An elongated void defines the heart of the museum, where a ramp connects the entrance level to the galleries.

Below left and right There is no single prescribed route through the building, rather a multiple choice of lifts, stairs and ramps allows visitors to create their own itinerary.

Opposite Detail view of the glazing to the north façade.

Below Top to bottom: Two cross-sections of the art galleries; north-west elevation; longitudinal section.

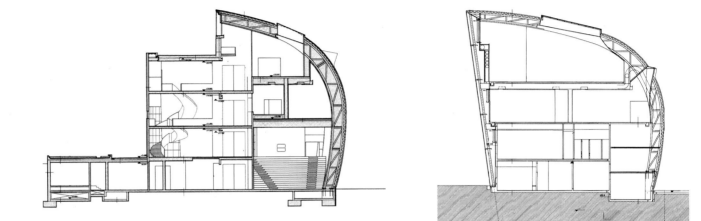

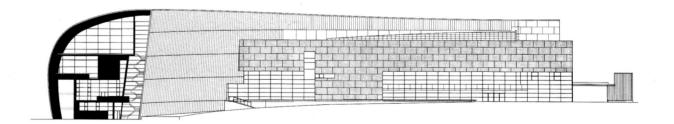

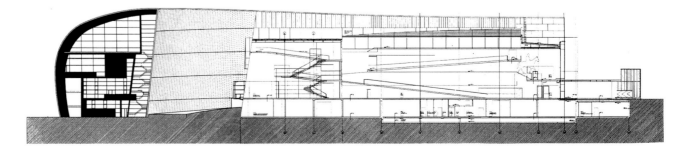

Left Concept sketch – the tripartite composition consists of a timber box framed above and below by translucent glass.

Opposite The entrance to the gallery is via an aluminium door, the only interruption in the fully-glazed band at ground level.

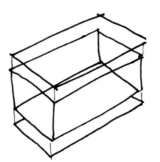

Goetz Collection Munich, Germany 1994

Architects
Herzog & de Meuron

Client
Ingvild Goetz

Programme
Art gallery
Library
Drawing storage

Location
The gallery stands in a secluded birch grove between a road and a 1960s residence that forms part of the same property. The gallery is placed so that it can be used either as a private or a public gallery, a decision that will be addressed at some time in the future.

Site Description
Arranged over three floors, the gallery building takes the form of a tripartite composition. A long timber box faced in birch ply, is separated from the ground by a band of glass, and crowned by another wider band of the same opaline-white, translucent glass. The apparently weightless box is suspended between the two bands of glass, generating a juxtaposition between transparency and opacity that typifies the architecture of Herzog & de Meuron. The galleries themselves occupy the upper and basement levels with a double-height entrance space wedged between them.

Building Solution
The Goetz Collection is an internationally renowned private collection of contemporary art. The collection's activities embrace the entire diversity of today's artistic forms of expression in all media. Apart from drawings, graphics, paintings and photography, the focus is on video and film work, room-sized installations and multichannel projections. The apparent simplicity of the building designed to house this important collection is derived from the building regulations that apply to the residential area that restricted the height and footprint of the building, making it necessary to construct a basement level to provide the required amount of exhibition space. Herzog & de Meuron turned this constraint into the basis for their design. The first step was to deliberately avoid the traditional solution of putting video art and drawings down in the basement, and to aim instead at achieving equal spatial quality on both exhibition levels. The conventional hierarchy of rooms is turned about. In this way, the usually top-lit main exhibition hall, which is the focus of many galleries, was placed in the basement. In the upper storey are three additional exhibition rooms. Within this unusual arrangement, the aim was to achieve equal spatial and light qualities on both exhibition levels.

The entrance to the gallery is via a door made from a panel of aluminium neatly framed by aluminium posts, and is the only interruption in the otherwise fully glazed band at ground level. In the entrance space, consisting of hallway, office and library, the visitor is still in contact with the garden which can be viewed through expansive, clear glazed doors. Two openings, symmetrically arranged in a partition wall, serve as access to two parallel flights of stairs, one leading to the upper floor and one to the basement.

The upper floor contains three identical, square exhibition spaces with walls of white-plastered brickwork designed to act as a neutral field on which to hang paintings. Each room is surmounted by bands of opaline glass that let natural daylight into the galleries without allowing views out. The apparently hermetically sealed, although softly and sympathetically lit, galleries act as a perfect foil for the attributes of the art collection contained within. The collection, accumulated over 30 years from the 1960s to the present, includes works by Bruce Naumann, Cy Twombly, Robert Ryman and Helmut Federle.

Descending to the basement, a darkened room containing a drawing-storage cabinet gives way to an exhibition space with the same glass bands and the same quality of natural light as the upper galleries. The identical nature of the galleries on the upper floor and in the basement, together with the

deliberate absence of any visual connection to the exterior, has a disorientating effect, causing the visitor to question the initial perception of a simple layered mass that was perceived from the exterior. As a result, the modest building, measuring only 24.2 metres long by 8 metres wide (79 by 26 feet), acquires an unexpected labrynthian complexity. Simultaneously it acts as an insular, interiorized world dedicated to the viewing of works of art.

The paradoxical character of the building is determined primarily by the glass, which is employed here not simply as a transparent or reflecting material – although, being glass, it also has these properties. Here, it is used as a three-dimensional screen that absorbs rather than reflects images from the exterior: a field of 'halation'. This photographic phenomenon, derived from the word 'halo' is defined as the spreading of light beyond its proper boundary. Architecturally, in the case of the Goetz Gallery, the term is apt. The glass bands are, in fact, formed from an inner and outer layer of glass, held 50 centimetres (20 inches) apart. This depth also corresponds to the dimension that separates the outer layer of birch ply from the interior walls of rendered brickwork. Within this hidden space, all

the elements that contribute to the practical workings of the building – rain gutters, electrical wiring, air circulation systems – are concealed so that the glass is able to take on the complexity of a three-dimensional spatial entity. As such the glass, the green tint of which was selected from 14 samples to harmonize with the colour of the grass, absorbs images of the exterior rather than simply reflecting them, in effect creating a halo of light crowning each of the galleries. This imparts what Jacques Herzog describes as 'a physical sense to the light reaching across the space'.

The result is that the gallery interiors are responsive to changing light while offering an almost constant environment in which to view the artworks. By contrast, the exterior is strangely elusive, appearing sometimes as a frieze animated by the movement of the reflections of trees and the changing sky. However as the hours and seasons change, the band can appear to dissolve into nothingness. Whatever the exterior condition or the changefulness of the façades when viewed from the garden, this building, monumental in scale and abstract in composition, allows nothing to distract from the contemplation of art.

Below left Detail view of the junction between the ground floor glazing and the timber cladding.

Below right Corner detail of the translucent glazing.

Opposite The three identical top-floor galleries are connected via simple portal openings. The simple white-plastered walls act as a neutral field on which to hang works of art.

Opposite View of the gallery at night through the birch grove that surrounds the building. The library, visible on the ground floor, is connected to the garden via large expanses of clear glazing.

Below Top to bottom: Upper-floor plan; ground-floor plan; basement-floor plan; elevation; longitudinal and cross-sections.

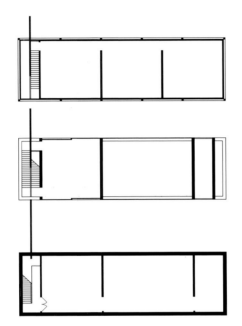

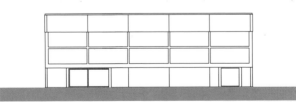

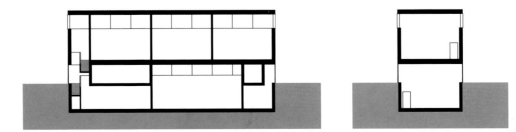

Left Concept sketch – the building solution is essentially a glass cube held between two glass screens.

Opposite The screens extend several metres beyond the top of the building, diffusing the edge against the sky.

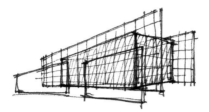

Fondation Cartier
Paris, France
1994

Architects
Jean Nouvel
Emanuel Cattani & Associates

Client
Gan Vie, COGEDIM

Programme
Contemporary art foundation
Cartier S.A. offices
Exhibition spaces

Location
The Fondation Cartier is located on the boulevard Raspail, Montparnasse, Paris, and was built on the site of the former American Cultural Centre, beginning in 1991 and completing in 1994.

Site Description
The site created a number of specific constraints on the new scheme, such as an adherence to the previous building lines, and also the incorporation of a 100-year-old cedar tree planted by Chateaubriand, together with the retention of the other existing trees.

These parameters influenced the subsequent space planning of the new building – programmatically defined as the headquarters for Cartier, exhibition spaces for a new modern art foundation, and accompanying administration and office spaces.

Building Solution
Jean Nouvel's architectural solution is essentially a glazed cube – a 'house of glass' caught visually between two large parallel screens. However, the building's basic 'H' footprint camouflages the overall net effect of the architectural form, and its true critical and at times intimate dialogue with the site context. For in front of the first screen, the main

façade of the foundation, is a third lower screen parallel to the building cube, but also adjacent to the boulevard Raspail. This intermediate surface 'frames' the single feature of the historic cedar tree, forming, in the process, an implied gateway into the complex. Caught between the visual interplay promoted by these three screens, the visitor to the foundation passes through and beneath the cedar and enters the exhibition spaces at ground-floor level. The architectural elements, in this way, support an urban choreography, providing a scenographic performance of static and dynamic forces. As Nouvel has commented, 'Blurring boundaries … the building becomes a refracting series of superimpositions of sky, trees and virtual (or reflected) trees.'

The presence and sense of proximity one has to the surrounding trees is continued inside the building because the exhibition spaces match the height of the main 8 metre (26 foot) high fenestration, providing a fully glazed elevation which is able to slide back in summer and allow the exhibitions to become a natural extension of the enclosing landscape. The top storeys of the foundation's front and rear façades are also extended by several metres, at the level of the roof terrace, so as to

diffuse the building's upper boundary edge against the sky, emphasizing, as Nouvel has put it, 'an architectural game of denying a reading of a solid volume. It is the poetic evanescence, creating an area where the pleasures of the magnificent garden, of trees and the art of the combined.'

The building itself is constructed from an eight-storey fine steel frame (with an additional seven storeys extending below ground), clad in aluminium frame and glass panels. The glass is comprised of anti-reflection double glazing, featuring external 12 millimetre (½ inch) laminated safety glass with a 10 metre (33 foot) cavity, and internally with 6 millimetre (¼ inch) float glass for the casement area, and 6 millimetre (¼ inch) toughened safety glass in the apron-wall area. Ground and basement floors, flooded with light, reinforcing the flowing transition between inside and outside, are reserved for exhibition spaces, while the seven storeys above them accommodate office and reception areas, with the top, eighth floor, containing a roof garden. The remaining six floors below ground are reserved for car parking, accessed via a car lift.

The main elevation of the building's transparent façade is comprised of a

post-and-rail frame, while the upper floors consist of all-glass elements in a structural sealant system articulated by a fine network of stainless-steel bars that provide the mechanical means of securing the construction. The bars also support the external sunblinds, installed independently at each storey and computer controlled. On the upper levels the inner partitions are also of glass, sand-blasted to eye level, with gradual transition above. The ground surface is neutralized against the reflection of the glass, being made up of granite and steel grating.

Below From the interior the steel frame becomes more apparent, without creating a visual barrier between the art gallery and the surrounding gardens.

Top The exceptional clarity of the anti-reflective glass, combined with the filigree steelwork creates a mass of overlayed shadows, inside and out.

Bottom The verticality of the steelwork in the ground-floor gallery mimics that of the trees in the gardens.

Opposite The elegant eight-storey-high steel frame becomes apparent only when the crystalline reflections of surrounding trees dissolve at close quarters.

Following pages Nouvel's intention was to play 'an architectural game of denying a reading of a spatial volume'.

Opposite The boulevard Raspail façade – at first, the glass screen appears to herald the building envelope. In fact, it delineates an open entrance courtyard featuring an historic cedar tree.

Below Top to bottom: Gallery floor plan; office-level floor plan; site plan; section – deceptively, there is almost as much of the building below ground as above it.

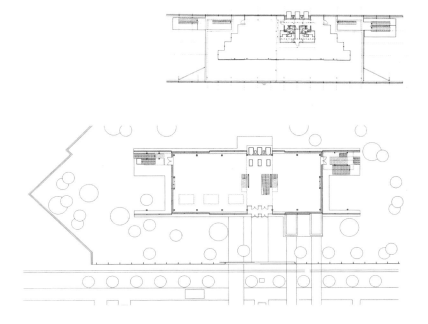

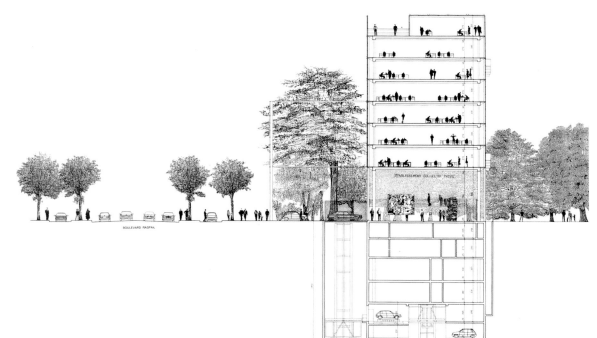

Left Concept sketch – the simple pavilion, constructed entirely from glass, minimizes its presence in the company of the historic Grade II listed Broadfield House.

Opposite The simplicity of the exterior belies the impressive feat of glass engineering the building represents – it is the largest all-glass structure in the world.

Broadfield House Glass Museum Dudley, UK 1994

Architects
Design Antenna

Client
Metropolitan Borough of Dudley

Programme
Glass museum
Entrance pavilion
Glass-blowing studio
New galleries

Location

Broadfield House Glass Museum is located in the small village of Kingswinford near Dudley, in the West Midlands of England. The area was once renowned for its industrial landscape of coal-burning brick-furnace cones, and canals for transporting raw materials, which produced the very best of seventeenth- and eighteenth-century English crystal glass (the famous Stourbridge glass industry once competed with the best of Venetian glass and the town was the centre of glass manufacture in England from the sixteenth century). Broadfield House is a Georgian Grade II listed property, originally the residence of the local squire and more recently connected to nearby Himley Hall, the former country estate of the Earl of Dudley, set in over 81 hectares (200 acres) of Capability Brown-designed landscape.

Site Description

The site is a secluded mature greenfield plot within the heart of Kingswinford, surrounded by small-scale residential properties, mature trees and hedgerows. The original house was sited towards the front portion of the plot, with a southerly orientation accessed directly off the adjacent main road. It initially consisted of a simple house that then underwent

successive gentrification and alterations, and in so doing became more significant through its architectural detail. As part of this later remodelling, the main entrance was dramatically reoriented from a south to a northern elevation, with the latter providing a carriage drive and longer route to the stylized portico, flanking Georgian windows and formal elevation.

More recently, in 1993, the house underwent extensive refurbishment, and the addition of a major glass extension, as part of a two-phase plan by the borough of Dudley to consolidate and rehouse several important collections of seventeenth- and eighteenth-century British glass. Phase I entailed the unification of the collection under one roof, while the second phase constituted a national architectural competition to found a new National Glass Museum of British Glass at Himley Hall.

The 'new' scheme for Broadfield consisted of an extensive brief for visitor facilities, the enhancement of exhibition displays, the addition of glass galleries, the establishment of a hot-glass studio for artists in residence, and the restoration of the main entrance to the southern elevation (by rerouting the internal planning of the building) by the

addition of an all-glass pavilion. The pavilion forms the main feature of the scheme, still believed to be the largest all-glass structure in the world. Representing a significant technical feat in contemporary glass engineering, the scheme also offers a powerful metaphor on the mythology of glass – dematerializing space and defying gravity through the conscious manipulation of light and shadow, while merging exterior and interior through the transparent glass envelope of the building's structure.

Building Solution

The architectural treatment of the building is to create a contemporary foil to the historic house and the glass collection within, as well as to provide an expression of the contemporary exploitation of modern glass technology, referencing, as it does, the early glass pioneers in Paul Scheerbart's visions of a new glass architecture and Mies van der Rohe's evocative renderings for his all-glass Berlin skyscraper. The new pavilion, in this way, is an essay on the all-transparent structure. It is a structure that merges the envelope: walls into roof, sky to ground, exterior to interior.

The glass envelope itself is presented as a pure glass box – an 'engineered' glass

Right The pavilion forms the entrance to the new National Glass Museum of British Glass at Himley Hall. At night the building glows, announcing its presence in the context of the dark masonry of the historic building to which it is attached.

structure with no visible metal supports or connectors. The structure itself is 11 metres long by 3.5 metres high by 5.3 metres wide (36 by 11.5 by 17.4 feet), based on a 1.1 metre (3.6 foot) structural module. Materially, it consists of a triple-glazed roof and double-glazed main elevation. The glass beams and finned columns are formed from three sheets of float glass laminated together to form structural frames, all jointed using simple mortice and tenon connections then bonded by silicone.

This glass envelope provides a dynamic synergy between aesthetic requirements and the resolution of climatic and environmental control. This was a significant factor in the final success of the design, because the pavilion faces south-west, is not air-conditioned, and had the potential to become a tinted or reflective box with the possibility that it would overheat. The solution to these inherent problems was formulated with French glass company Saint Gobain and their application of Cool-Lite-Neutral KN169 – a specific soft coating to the inner panes that has the attributes of insulation, but also enhances the quality and transparency of light within the contained space. This is largely applied to the inner face of the outer pane of the roof glazing and the vertical wall panels.

Manufactured at Saint Gobain's factory in Holland, Neutral KN169 is specially coated glass that has a microscopic deposit of silver layered onto its surface to inhibit solar gain. This metallic tinting has the advantage over other manufactured glass that it is highly transparent, and although slightly tinted this is not readable to the eye. The glass was supplied toughened for safety, 10 millimetres (⅖ inch) thick for the roof and 8 millimetres (⅓ inch) thick for the wall cladding. The vertical glazing permits 45 per cent of the solar energy to enter the space, while maintaining 61 per cent of the natural daylight. To enhance the specific performance of the roof panels, the inner pane was also supplied with a white screen-printed pattern fused onto the surface in the form of a gridded frit pattern. The density of this pattern was varied to reduce the solar energy entering the building to less than 37 per cent, with the frit acting as an integral solar reflector over the surface area of the roof. The resultant structure offers high environmental performance with a U value of 1.7w/sqm, while providing a minimal degree of external reflection and a high level of light transmission.

Opposite Interior of the glass exhibition spaces.

Below The architects resolved the potential for solar gain (the building faces south-west) by utilizing a technically sophisticated coating with microscopic deposits of silver that acts as insulation without compromising the quality of the transparency.

Opposite Light fittings are incorporated seamlessly into the line of the silicon joints used to fix the glass elements in place.

Below Top to bottom: Site plan – Broadfield House was originally a Georgian property located in over 81 hectares (200 acres) of landscaped grounds; ground-floor plan.

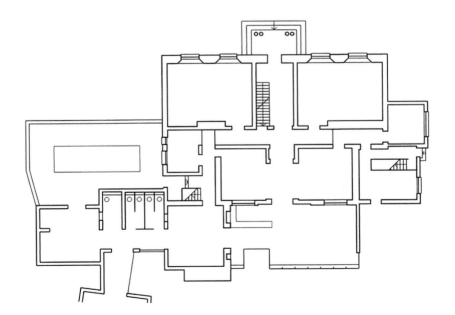

Left Concept sketch – a new glass block offers a complete contrast to the old palace, with its classical 'C'-shaped plan, as well creating the 'missing' fourth wing.

Opposite A ceramic fritted pattern creates a silvery matrix across the surface of the façade.

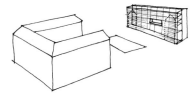

The Museum of Art
Lille, France
1997

Architects
Jean Marc Ibos
Myrto Vitart

Client
Musée des Beaux Arts, Cité de Lille

Programme
New gallery
Office
Visitor facilities

Location

The original Musée des Beaux Arts building was built 1892 in the city of Lille, France, and contains one of the most important collections of art in France. The site is dominated by the existing historic building, the old palace, which is formed in a symmetrical, classical 'C' plan, with three principal wings around a central courtyard, with the fourth side closed by a connecting roofed colonnade.

Site Description

The project to refurbish the museum was initiated to give the old palace a new and grander appearance, and to redress the various earlier and previous historic additions. The new scheme, which began construction in 1993 and was completed in 1997, opens up the existing building towards the city centre without impairing its visual integrity. This older structure is enlivened by sympathetic restoration while the new addition offers a contrasting and wholly contemporary approach – 'an impressionistically alienated form' as Jean Marc Ibos describes it, that reflects the historic integrity of its site and the existing building in a fresh way, so that the new building acquires an 'immaterial quality'.

Building Solution

Ibos and Vitart's response to the dominant Beaux Arts palace is to create the missing fourth elevation as a largely transparent wing set to one side of, but adjacent to, the central courtyard, in the form of a full-height glass-clad elevation. The new wing, in this way, is formulated as a free-standing six-storey flank of accommodation, which reflects and provides a foil of transparency between the old and new buildings.

This new façade is presented as a flat double-glazed envelope comprising 416 panels, the outer panes of which are set flush and mirrored on their inner face, while a ceramic frit pattern is expressed as a silver-gridded matrix. Behind the elevation, the internal spaces are revealed as a long corridor, the face of which creates a vivid backdrop to the scheme, and is painted in crimson interspersed with a series of large gold rectangles. Amid this dramatic use of colour, the façade offers a highly specific visual game of light interplay, colour and reflection. Within this game, the glazed wall is manipulated by the response of the reflected images on its surface while the light is purely reflected back, giving the impression of depth and layering of space over all six levels of the building. The total effect is a kaleidoscope of colour and light, generating a rarefied mirage of images that reflect and refract to subvert the visitor's perception of the space. According to the architects, 'The building is a mirror of reality. It is a reflector that explores the meaning of presence, materiality, absence, and tests our sense of place.'

To heighten this effect, the edge of the roof of the office wing is detailed in a very precise manner – sloping back sharply away from the parapet line and the plane of the glass façade, so as to conceal the main roof from eye level when viewed from the ground. The net effect is that the wall appears as an incredibly minimal surface, a unified sheet of translucency, rather than simply being the elevation to the extension.

The construction of the double-glazed façade is comprised of an outer layer of 12 millimetre (½ inch) toughened safety glass (with a 15 millimetre (⅝ inch) air cavity) and an inner layer of 12 millimetre (½ inch) laminated safety glass. Both systems are supported and held in place by a series of polished stainless-steel posts, with fixings, also in stainless steel, hinged in the pane of the glass.

Below and in front of the office wing, under a large 720 square metre (7,750

Below The façade is a dramatic composition of light and colour. Behind the glazed wall, a crimson- and gold-painted wall lends additional depth to the reflective nature of the fritted glazing.

Opposite The highly patterned glass façade nonetheless creates a perfect surface on which to reflect the surrounding historic buildings.

square foot) glazed roof, are the new exhibition spaces and a subterranean link to the older building. Lighting these spaces below, the roof is laid flush with the paving of the surrounding square, giving the appearance of a reflective lake of water. The perimeter of this surface is surrounded by an edging of water to prevent direct pedestrian access onto the actual roof, while the glass itself is supported by a grid of six aluminium-clad channel sections fixed to a primary grid of steel beams. On the internal, underside of this canopy, adjustable aluminium louvres are able to mediate the extent of light entering into the galleries, while above, the roof acts as a large-scale mirror that conspires to make the overall impression of the building more visually challenging, capturing both the image of the new wing while reflecting the changing light of the sky above.

Right and opposite The 416 panels of laminated double-glazing are held in place with a series of polished stainless-steel posts and fixings.

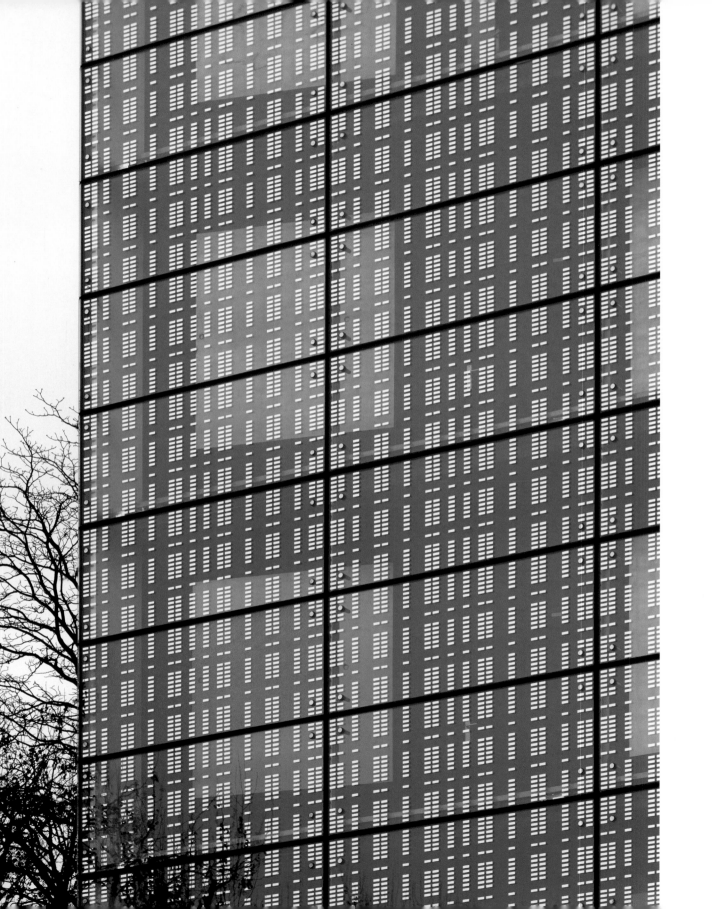

Opposite The layering of patterned glass with the attendant reflections lend the building an immaterial quality, providing a foil for the dignified presence of the palace.

Below Top to bottom: Site plan of the palace (left) showing the slim footprint of the new wing on the right; floor plan; section through the courtyard illustrating the slim profile of the new addition.

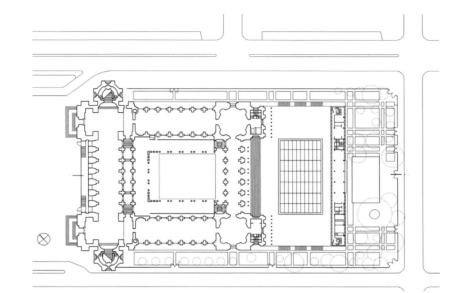

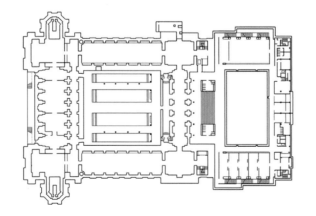

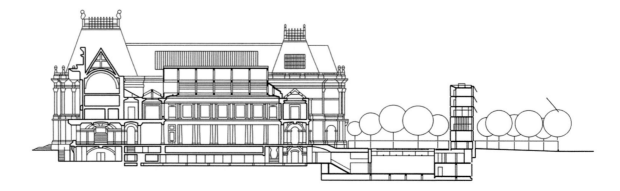

Left Concept sketch – seven 'bottles of light' emerge from a stone box.

Opposite Aerial view – at the corner of a reflection pool, entitled 'the thinking field', a bell tower heralds the chapel's presence on the campus.

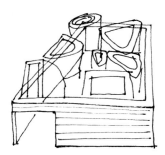

Chapel of Ignatius
Seattle, USA
1997

Architects
Steven Holl Architects

Client
Seattle University

Programme
Chapel
Processional ramp
Bell tower
Reflection pool

Location
Seattle University, on the west coast of the United States, is a Jesuit institution in the 450-year-old Ignatian tradition. Founded in 1891 and located in the heart of downtown Seattle, the university is home to 6,000 undergraduate and graduate students. The new Jesuit chapel is embodied into the campus of the university, which was originally planned to conform to the existing urban block network of the city. A series of new green quadrangles located to the north, south, west and east bring a renewed sense of collegiate identity to the campus, reinforced by the location of the chapel on the south-east corner of the eastern quadrangle. The site itself is located in close proximity to the halls of residence, the student union and campus services buildings.

Site Description
In 1991 the president of the university commissioned a new chapel dedicated to St Ignatius that would not only enhance the religious lives of the students, but would serve the spiritual needs of the wider community. The chapel is sited on the north–south axis of the campus, flanked on all sides by green quadrangles. The grassed area to the south, while inhabited by the students as an integral part of the

campus' landscaped space, is nonetheless an important part of the immediate context of the chapel, along with a shallow reflection pool, entitled 'the thinking field'. At the junction of the pool and the quadrangle a bell tower heralds the presence of the chapel amid the distractions and activity of the campus.

Building Solution
The design reflects a period of intensive research undertaken by the architect, in which he engaged with Jesuit liturgy to produce a concept that embraces St Ignatius' *Spiritual Exercises*, which was written as a guide-book to personal prayer and spiritual awareness. The building is conceived as a 'gathering of different lights', referring to the diversity of the students who have come from all over the world, and to the programme of liturgical procession that moves through a series of places of prayer. The image also reinforces the idea of students and teachers examining ideas in different lights, as well as the use of the 'light of reason' to understand complex issues.

The gathering of lights was subsequently developed into 'seven bottles of light' emerging from a 'stone box'. Emerging from the 'stone box' of the chapel, constructed from 21

interlocking concrete tilt-up slabs, each steel-framed 'bottle' expresses an element of the Jesuit liturgical programme: the procession hall; the narthex; the main gathering space; the reconciliation chapel; the choir; the chapel of the Blessed Sacrament; and the seventh 'bottle' – the bell tower, reflected in the pool. Each of these vessels illuminates a place of ritual and spirituality. Each individually shaped 'bottle' filters light through a coloured glass lens which is then reflected off a painted surface in a complementary colour located opposite each lens, concealed by baffles so that only the reflected colour can be seen from within the chapel.

On entering the chapel the first vessel is the processional corridor, filled with natural south light and with a gently sloped floor that takes the worshipper up towards higher ground. To the right is the second vessel, the narthex, where people gather before and after services and where five paintings depict the life and spiritual journey of St Ignatius. The main sanctuary where the congregation gathers for worship catches the strongest light and is distinguished by a blue lens and a yellow field to the east and a yellow lens with a blue field to the west. The choir is illuminated through a

red lens reflected off a green field, while the chapel of the Blessed Sacrament – a small room where the Eucharistic bread from the Mass is reserved for distribution to the sick – is lit through a purple lens reflected off an orange field.

By manipulating colour as well as the intensity and directionality of the light, each space is imbued with a distinct atmosphere without the overt use of architectural ornament. The manipulation of daylight is reversed at night when each volume is lit from within, turning each of the 'bottles' into a glowing coloured beacon, visible across the campus. The use of complementary colours in each window opening is explained by the architect as the 'two-fold merging of concept and phenomena' – which in effect is more dramatic than stained glass and more nuanced than single-coloured windows. The reality of this duality can be experienced by staring at, for example, a blue rectangle of light and then at a white surface. A yellow rectangle will appear to the viewer.

For Holl, glass is used not just as a building material or simply as a way of expressing an architectural concept. For him, glass is a far more subtle carrier of meaning, both architectural (the architect's interpretation of the Jesuit liturgy), and as a material that will have a life of its own after it has been locked into place as part of the permanent fabric of the chapel. For example, time and duration are also expressed through the glazing – when clouds pass between the sun and the chapel, a 'phenomenal pulse' of reflected colour occurs, invigorating the space and making observers aware of the broader context of their surroundings. This architectural expression of phenomena such as 'light', 'time' and 'space' is, on one level, a creative function of the interpretation of an earthly brief, and more than serves its purpose of creating an uplifting, sacred space for this Jesuit chapel. On the other hand, it also interprets with an incredible exactitude the words of St Augustine (AD 354–430), when he speculates about the nature of time: 'What then is time? If no one asks me, I know. If I want to explain it to a questioner, I do not know. We measure time, but how can we measure what does not exist? The past is no longer, the future is not yet, the present has not duration. When I measure time I measure impressions, modifications of consciousness.'

Below left Each of the seven spaces within the building has its own colour identity. Light filters through a glass lens which is reflected off a concealed painted surface located opposite each lens.

Below right The plaster-finished walls in the chapel are the perfect surface for reflecting the soft light diffused through the rooftop lenses.

Opposite In the chapel occasional slots of clear glazing reveal glimpses of the exterior.

Opposite While the interior is, for the most part, inward-looking, subtle connections with the world outside occur when, for example, a cloud passes over, temporarily dimming the soft coloured light inside.

Below Top to bottom left: Floor plan; longitudinal section. Top to bottom right: cross-sections.

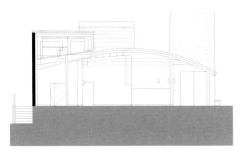

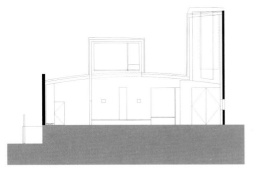

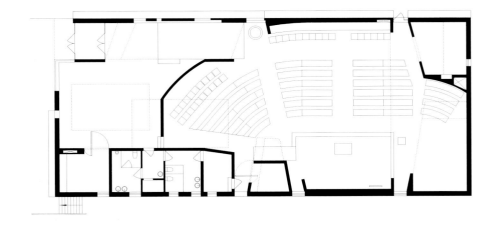

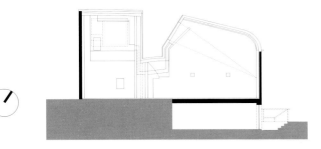

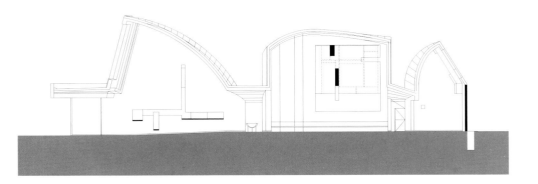

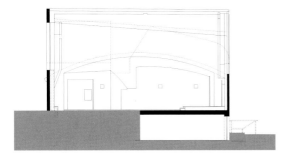

Left Concept sketch – the buiding is arranged as a simple orthogonal form, out of which the dominant form of the concert hall rises.

Opposite The concert hall rises above the glass box of the entrance foyer, dominating the architectural composition.

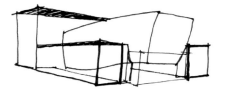

Concert Hall
St Pölten, Austria
1997

Architects
Klaus Kada

Client
NÖ Hypo Leasing
Grundstücksvermietungs GmbH

Programme
Concert hall
Chamber music hall
Theatre
Rehearsal rooms
Bar
Restaurant
Administration facilities

Location
Located in St Pölten, an industrial and college city 60 kilometres (37 miles) west of Vienna, the concert hall forms a 'hinge' in the new cultural district that connects St Pölten's government district with the baroque and late nineteenth-century centre of this up-and-coming city of 50,000 inhabitants. In 1986 the city was elected the new capital of Lower Austria, which since the end of the monarchy had been governed by Vienna despite the fact that it was Austria's largest federal state. As a symbol of the new order and a gesture of confidence in the future, an architectural competition was held to design a cultural quarter for the city, of which the concert hall is a centrepiece.

Site Description
The complex is arranged as a simple, low-lying form out of which the dominant form of the glass concert hall rises, expressing an interpretation of the brief in which the priority of musical performance is given 'centre stage'. Working within the constraints of the Hans Hollein masterplan for the area, Kada accepted a conventionally symmetrical parallel-sided form, harnessing his ingenuity as a designer to make the space as flexible as possible. The concert hall's unusual form permits

it to host operas, ballets, musicals and plays. The complex also has a practice stage and a chamber music hall.

Building Solution
The building was originally orientated to serve as an arrival and meeting point for a new *Landhaus* boulevard (country house boulevard), close to the commercial and retail district, which is arranged as a sequence of streets and squares. However, in order to fit in with Hans Hollein's masterplan (developed as part of the city's competition for the new cultural district), the building was later turned through 90 degrees and moved to the western edge of the complex where it would serve as a hinge between the old and new parts of the city.

While the body of the hall originally sat more casually in an outer framework of circulation zones and secondary areas, the volume was gradually developed using increasingly precise models and computer studies to develop the organically amorphous form. As a result, the inner curves of the acoustic and optical shell became a compact form rising up out of the fly-tower.

Kada's vision for the concert hall was to create an enormous 'open house', out of which the main auditorium would be

singled out as a 'shining crystal' making the entire complex physically and symbolically visible. The architect compares this approach to the organization of a circus tent, which is brightly lit, towering above the fairground, while the wagons and other service areas cluster around the edges, almost as if they were 'docked' to the base of the tent.

Dominating the composition, the enormous mass of the auditorium creates a visual fulcrum around which all of the connecting spaces are arranged. Constructed as a concrete shell curved in two directions, the auditorium floats above the orthogonal planes and rectilinear volumes below. Its apparent weightlessness is generated by the cladding of back-lit translucent glass that covers the form like a stretched skin. Due to the complex geometry and minimal tolerances of the glass shell, laser technology, directly controlled by a computer program, was used to survey the substructure and the cutting of the glass panels, each of which is, despite initial impressions, flat.

The glass panels hang on a network of cables anchored to the edges of the eaves, and at various points braced against the concrete wall with

compression rods. Enough room remains between the concrete shell and the glass skin for narrow service walkways and batteries of floodlights. At night, light is reflected off the white-painted concrete and filtered through the translucent glass to produce a completely uniform light.

The glass cladding of the concert hall is separated from the solid roofs of the peripheral buildings by a continuous glazed rooflight of transparent glass spanning a void. This, more than anything else, produces the impression of a gap between the auditorium and the rationally structured outer wings, a gap in which the stairs and landings of the foyer occur like so many secondarily added bridges and connections. The gap also stresses the continuity between the glass cladding, which is able to be touched inside, but can only be seen outside. At night when the whole building is lit up, the space left around the auditorium seems to flow out into the square, leaving the body of the auditorium floating independent of the side pavilions.

The complex cellular organism that surrounds the great hall hugs the ground in contrast to the floating glass hull above. The greater width of the north wing was prompted by the presence at the third level and towards the west end of a small 250-seat concert hall. This, too, is a flexible space in terms of acoustics and lighting, used for lectures and readings as well as chamber concerts. Symmetrically opposite it on the other side of the stage areas are two rehearsal rooms, placed one above the other. Not being public rooms, their presence is not signalled externally. Visually, they are absorbed into a belt of offices and dressing rooms on seven levels, which wraps around the west of the building and round its south-west corner. As this is the back of the building it is treated in a rational and straightforward fashion with a regular glass curtain wall. Only the fly-tower looming above suggests that the building is a theatre.

Glass is used extensively throughout the complex to create a lucidity and floating lightness that characterizes the entire design. The *Kammersaal*, or chamber music hall, is clad in blue-glass shingles and raised on ultra-slim columns above the extravagantly glazed bar and restaurant, creating a strong presence on the northern façade facing the town. In addition, the minimalist service stair enclosure and, facing the main square of the cultural district, the large glass wall of the foyer dramatically interrupted by the curved prow of the concert hall floating above, utilize glass to celebrate their presence.

The process employed by Kada, of dividing up the programme, unravelling it to generate individual blocks of space, can be perceived throughout the project. Each block, representing a programmatic element, is placed at a distance, one from the other, then connected again with dramatically glazed transit areas used for circulation and internal day-lighting. Using the glass as a determining material, Kada has taken the theme of lucidity of structure, space, programme and movement to define the architecture and, by extension, the city.

Left and below Views of the concert hall by day and night. The mass of the hall creates a visual fulcrum around which all the secondary spaces are arranged. Its apparent weightlessness is created through the use of back-lit translucent glass.

Below The glass-clad concert hall is separated from the peripheral buildings by a glazed roof spanning a void that houses the stairs and landings of the foyer.

Opposite At night, light is reflected off the white-painted concrete shell and filters out through the translucent glazing to create a uniform glow.

Opposite Due to the complex double curve of the concert hall, the concrete substructure was surveyed by laser technology before a sophisticated computer program was used to cut the glass panels, each of which, despite appearances, is flat.

Below Top to bottom left: Site plan (1: concert hall); longitudinal section; cross-section. Top to bottom right: Second, first and ground floor plans.

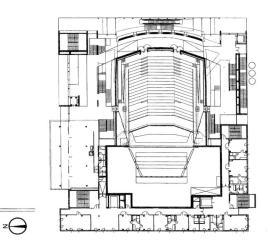

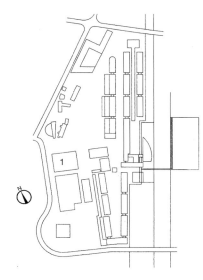

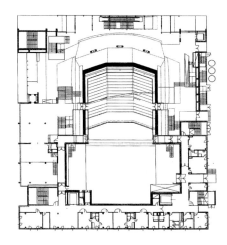

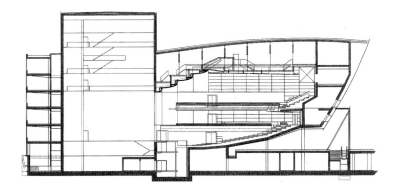

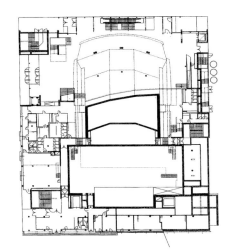

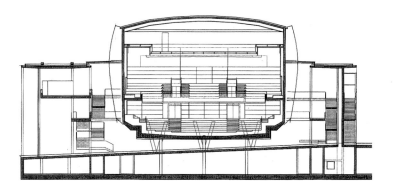

Left Concept sketch – the architectural response consists of a citrus grove enclosed behind a high stone wall.

Opposite A glass-walled band of accommodation is separated from the exterior wall by a linear terrace.

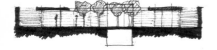

Balearic Technological and European Business Innovation Centre
Majorca, Spain
1998

Architects
Alberto Campo Baeza Architects

Client
Government of Balearics
Juan de Austria Vial 'C'

Programme
Business centre
Offices
Auditorium
Staff cafeteria
Computer facilities
Underground car park

Location
The Balearic Technological and European Business Innovation Centre is located at Inca, in the heart of Majorca off the eastern coast of Spain, on a flat central plain in the foothills of the Tramuntana mountain range. Inca, the principal town of the Es Raiguer region, is an artisan centre, historically renowned for leather craftsmanship.

Site Description
The centre is situated on a triangular site within a nondescript industrial park, where the sprawling clutter of factories, showrooms and billboards has had a dominant influence on the architectural response. Campo Baeza's project, won in competition in 1995, houses development agencies operating at local, Balearic and European levels. With an emphasis on information technology, the building is designed to act as a symbol of confidence for the future of the island's technological expertise.

Building Solution
The architectural response to the semi-urban, semi-industrial site was to separate it from its context by enclosing a citrus grove behind high stone walls to create a calm courtyard garden. The walls are constructed from blocks of *piedra mares*, a local sandstone, and

lined with travertine marble that continues across the ground plane to create, as the architects describe it, 'a travertine box open to the sky'. A 6 by 6 metre (20 by 20 foot) grid is traced across the horizontal surface of the box, providing a Cartesian logic for the placement of both structure and landscape elements.

Pedestrian access from the street is via a gentle ramp and adjacent steps along a short façade before it turns a 45-degree corner back along the south-facing hypotenuse. The slight shift in alignment of this entrance façade creates a semi-public space where visitors orient themselves before moving into the inner sanctum.

Separated from the inside face of the external wall by a slot of linear terrace that is open to the sky, a band of accommodation comprised of offices, meeting rooms, classrooms and a cafeteria, wraps around the perimeter. This band is topped by a continuous roof plane floating overhead, cantilevering 2 metres (6.5 feet) on either side, and supported on cylindrical steel columns. The accommodation is separated into three discrete pavilions, with the junctions at the corners of the triangle acting as connecting spaces between

the internal courtyard and the perimeter walkway. The walls of the pavilions are created from sheer panes of full-height, frameless glass. On the face closest to the external wall the columns are located inside the glass, while on the courtyard side the columns are placed on the exterior, creating the impression of a finely attenuated cloister around the perimeter of the garden.

This appealingly simple arrangement is made possible as a result of raising the entire podium above natural ground level and excavating a basement underneath in which to house spaces not in need of constant daylight, such as computer resources, a 110-seat auditorium and a parking garage. The only hint of this secretive lower floor is the stairwells located at the angles of the triangular plan, and the small square openings at the perimeter that allow for clerestory lighting and air extract.

Glass is used here in the simplest of ways – as a 'glass box' in the best modernist tradition. What differs here is that light is recognized as a transforming factor, in the way the glazing is perceived. Sandwiched between the deep eaves of the overhanging roof and the uninterrupted plane of the travertine floor, the glass effortlessly separates the

two horizontal elements while appearing to be as insubstantial as a taut piece of fabric. The effect is heightened by the contrast between the intensity of the Mediterranean light that falls unchecked into the courtyard, and the deep shade cast by the roof, in which the glass appears weightless, reflectionless – in fact, to almost disappear.

Opposite The walls of the pavilion are made from sheer panes of full-height glass, with a deep roof overhang to create shaded, cool interior spaces.

Below The accommodation, consisting of offices, meeting rooms, classrooms and a cafeteria, wraps around the perimeter of the site.

Following pages Glass is used here in the modernist tradition – as a 'glass box'.

Opposite On the courtyard side the columns are placed outside the line of the glazing, creating a cloister around the citrus grove.

Below Interior of one of the meeting rooms.

Opposite Glass is used in the simplest of ways. Large full-height panes of silicon-jointed glass provide a counterpoint to the solidity of the stone and transform the way light and shadow act on the building.

Below Top to bottom: Axonometric view of the centre; north-west elevation; south elevation; longitudinal section.

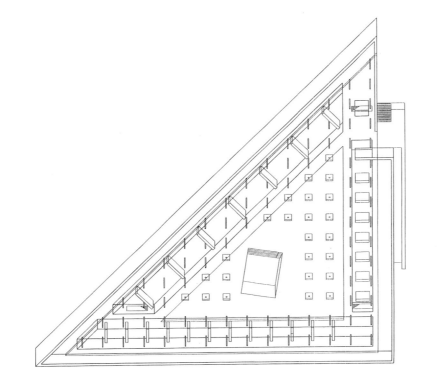

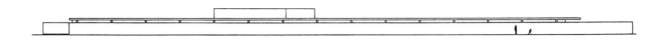

Opposite Concept sketch – a simple rectangular glass prism is raised on a black stone plinth.

Right Located on a historic site between the city and a park, the museum negotiates between the urban context and the natural landscape.

Museum Het Valkhof Nijmegen, The Netherlands 1998

Architects
UN Studio Architects

Client
Nijmegen Municipal Council

Programme
Contemporary museum
Gallery
Storage
Administration
Restaurant
Café auditorium
Education room
Library
Archive

Location

The Het Valkof Museum is located on a prominent historic site, close to the medieval city of Nijmegen and to Kelfenbos park, the city's oldest public landscaped space. The building negotiates between the urban context and the natural landscape, and is situated on a triangular site on a plateau which falls steeply down to the river Waal, with the town to the south, the park to the east, and with views to the north of nearby Roman ruins.

Site Description

Arranged over three floors, the museum building takes the form of a rectangular prism, clad with green-blue translucent panes of horizontal glazing, with small areas of clear glass, and mounted on a raised black stone plinth. The ground and basement levels house administrative functions and storage spaces, while the upper-floor museum and exhibition spaces occupy the raised first floor.

Building Solution

As a contemporary museum, the building represents a hybrid contemporary public meeting space, described by the architects as 'a mixture of supermarket, temple and tourist attraction'. In Nijmegen the architectural solution to this most contemporary of building types is integrated into a composite holistic form, responsive to changing activities. The building appears like a low hermetic structure that at night palpitates delicately through a glass outer skin, which dematerializes the building's horizontal mass and conceals a variety and richness of internal spaces within.

Movement organizes the structuring principle of the museum in two ways: the 15 metre (49 foot) wide staircase, which starts on the square in front of the museum and continues to the balcony zone on the upper level; and the ceiling, which follows the same route. Both elements serve several functions at once. The staircase functions as a public meeting place, as part of the load-bearing structure of the building and is also a distributor in the way that its branches shoot off to the various programmatic elements, such as the café, library, museum and central hall.

The ceiling, comprised of lightweight aluminium slats, is naturally lit from above to create a luminous ambience for the art and artefacts below. Like a blanket casually thrown over an object, the ceiling covers, but does not conceal or disguise, the multitude of installations for lighting and climate control, the labyrinth of wires, fixings, fittings, sprinklers and alarms. The wave-like structure varies according to the expected movement of visitors. In spaces where most people converge, the waves in the ceiling are more frequent, while they are less frequent and shallower in spaces where less climate-controlling machinery needs to be housed. These large compositional elements, the stair and ceiling, as well as the floor, are designed to communicate movement, to accompany visitors on their journey through the museum. Each surface is continuous in order to generate a flowing dynamic within a cohesive, inclusive whole.

This route, described simultaneously by the staircase and the ceiling, provides the architectural generator for the museum experience. The museum floor is divided into five spacious, parallel 'streets' over the whole width of the building. The strictly regulated pattern is interrupted by openings and cross-connections at different locations. This creates diagonal views through two, three or more rooms, enabling visitors to catch glimpses of what awaits them in neighbouring spaces and to meander among the archaeological artefacts and paintings at will via an unprescribed

Top right Exhibition and gallery space on the raised first floor.

Below right A 15 metre (49 foot) wide staircase constitutes the main structuring principle of the museum, and also functions as a public meeting place.

Opposite The glass façades appear as shimmering screens stretched across the surface of the building. The two long sides consist of transparent glass while the other two sides are translucent.

itinerary. In this way, the structured floor plan is challenged and deformed by the more fluid and dynamic human movement patterns.

The exterior of the building, however, reveals none of the spatial complexity of the interior – from the outside the museum consists of two boxes stacked one on top of the other: a rectangular base supporting a box with two skewed sides. The façades appear as stretched shimmering screens consisting partly of transparent glass (at the side and rear), with the remaining surfaces made up of translucent, milky glass. The abstraction of the synthetic blue glass envelope deliberately avoids any reference either to its context or to the contents of the museum. While abstract, it is not static – changes in the colour of the sky, the daylight and the seasons are communicated in the façades, which take on varying tones of grey, blue and green.

On the interior, however, the glass performs a function as important as the exhibits themselves. Using the glass, the landscape is taken up as an integral part of the interior of the museum, anchoring the building to its surroundings and contextualizing many of the artefacts that have been found nearby. At various

points around the perimeter of the museum, the space is deliberately kept free of artefacts in order that the glazing, and hence the view, take priority. In this way, the entire museum is conceived as a suite of frames through which the landscape is brought into the museum, thus turning the view into the museum's major exhibit.

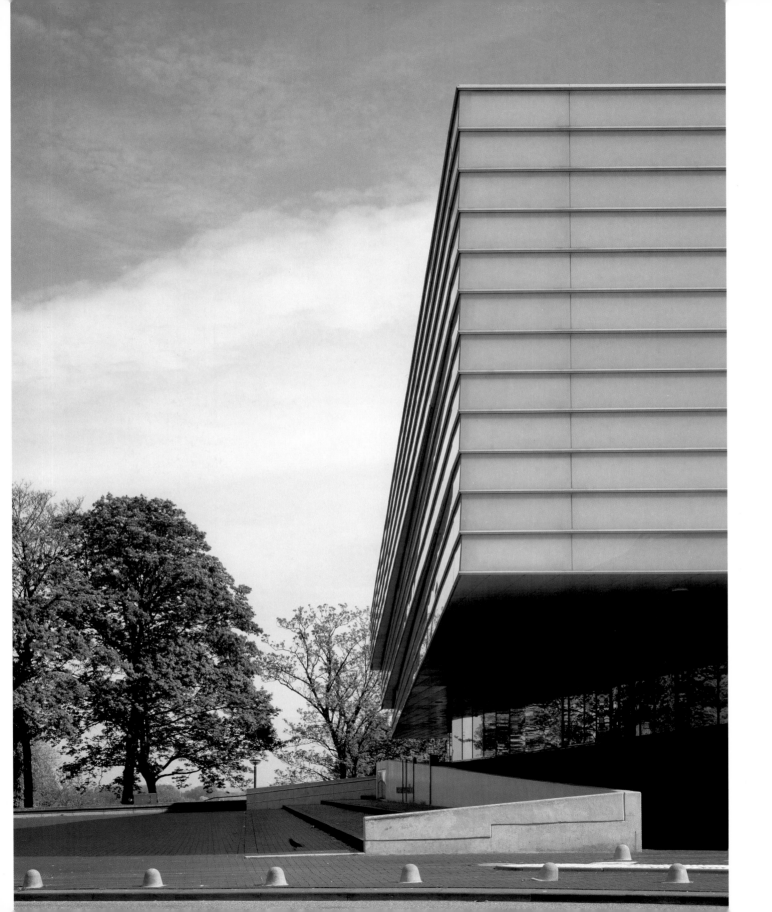

Below Through the glass, the surrounding landscape becomes an integral part of the interior of the museum.

Opposite Around the perimeter of the exhibition spaces artefacts are placed to deliberately make a visual connection between the objects and the landscape from which they came.

Opposite The horizontal mass of the building is articulated by a series of overhangs that traverse the long elevations of the building.

Below Top to bottom: Section; first-floor plan; ground-floor plans.

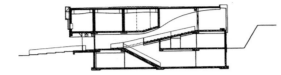

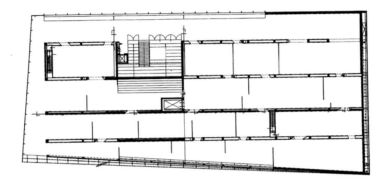

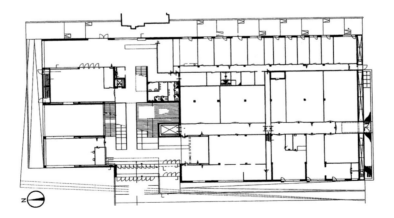

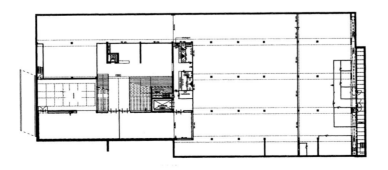

The Kursaal Centre San Sebastian, Spain 1999

Architects
Rafael Moneo Architects

Client
City of San Sebastian
Diputacion Foral of Guipuzcoa

Programme
Cultural and congress centre
Exhibition and assembly spaces
Banqueting hall

Location

The new Kursaal Centre, in the Basque city of San Sebastian, is situated alongside the dramatic natural backdrop of the city's north Atlantic coast – next to the mouth of the Urumea estuary, and adjacent to Mount Urgull and the arc of Concha Bay. Despite the proximity of these landscape elements, the site itself is essentially large and empty, without immediate scale and dominated by the scope of the Bay of Biscay. Seen in plan, the area offers a void block of land parallel to the coast, contained on either side by its sandy bay, yet opened up to the city behind by the incision of the nearby Urumea River, which penetrates the orthogonal grid of San Sebastian's urban form from its estuary by the sea.

Site Description

The site had formerly been occupied by a collection of earlier buildings which had been progressively abandoned during various economic downturns, so that by the mid-1990s all that was left was a tracery of building footprints concealed beneath a dense boundary of sea defences and anonymous street furniture. This meant that the site had lost its earlier connection to San Sebastian, leaving the edge of the city exposed to the elements, and the land, like a geographic incident, waiting for future transformation. For the architect Rafael Moneo, the geographic potential of the site immediately became a major inspiration for the new Kursaal Centre, and he sought in the finished building the idea of 'maintaining the condition of a topographic incident … and link with the natural landmarks of this part of the coast'.

Building Solution

Moneo's architectural response was 'to create two gigantic rocks washed ashore at the mouth of the Urumea River: not belonging to the city, they are rather part of the landscape.' This simple, yet powerful, concept offered the promise of not just another building for San Sebastian, but an architectural intervention as an almost natural feature of the landscape. Like the landscape, the building's silhouette is not tied into the urban fabric, but 'materializes as two crystalline volumes anchored in the sand, cubes that are not cubes, but figures sculpted with a surface of fluted glass, opaque and continuous'.

The Centre itself offers a neat composition of two methacrylate prisms (which at night become luminous solids) set within a new urban park. This open space is bordered at ground level by a continuous raised single-storey plinth which houses the substructure on three deeper levels (accommodating exhibition spaces, circulation, a restaurant, offices and dressing rooms). Above the plinth are two independent prismatic structures, approximately 20 metres (65.6 feet) high and orientated in different directions, the larger one housing the main auditorium and the smaller volume accommodating the congress hall. The plinth and load-bearing structures for each volume are constructed from reinforced concrete and precast elements, with random pieces of slate, 10 centimetres by 1.5 metres (4 inches by 5 feet), set within the cement. Against the solidity of these plinth elements, the halls are more lightweight, made with glass-clad steel, and forming nocturnally iridescent translucent envelopes.

The outer skin of these prisms is constructed from a series of curved laminated safety-glass panels, 25 centimetres by 6 centimetres (10 by 2.4 inches) – using reeded glass – fixed horizontally to concealed cast-aluminium glazing bars. This is then attached to a huge loadbearing welded sheet-steel skeleton frame, which is tilted vertically outwards at the narrower end of each hall layout. Inside, the inner skin is made up of flat 19 millimetre

Above Between the outer glass skin and the volume of the concert hall, stairways and landings provide access to the galleries and provide opportunities for people to gather.

Below The outer skin is comprised of curved safety-glass panels fixed to cast-aluminium glazing bars.

Opposite The two glass forms (the congress hall on the left and auditorium on the right) are placed lightly on the Atlantic coast of San Sebastian.

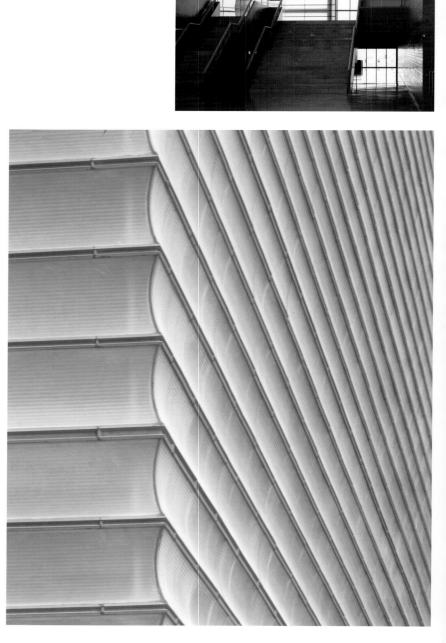

(¾ inch) sand-blasted float-glass panels. In contrast to the outer surfaces, the horizontal glazing bars of this inner skin are concealed by cedarwood cover strips to match the internal finishes. In both leaves, the vertical joints are sealed with silicone. Between the two skins, horizontal gangways facilitate the cleaning of the two planes from within the spaces. A few well-placed windows punctuate the façades, creating extended views out to sea, and also vistas to the backdrop of the coast.

Overall, the effect of the outer cladding is to generate a scale-like diffusion of light. Together with the ability of the surfaces to cast internal reflections during the day, at night, the two volumes are transformed into magical luminous objects, like two illuminated lanterns washed up by the seashore.

Like a number of earlier works by Moneo, the building plays with ambiguity, both in terms of the centre's materials and its construction. Simultaneously volumetric and transparent, the two prisms appear as two rocks. The curving of the glass evokes waves and foam as if to echo the nearby sea, while the glass is used both in an abstract and yet also highly material way.

Opposite Detail view of one of the stairways that traverse the dramatic, full-height interior space, apparently unsupported as they butt seamlessly into the translucent glass walls.

Below Detail view of the curved glass panels in the context of San Sebastian's historic old town.

Following pages At night the two methacrylate prisms become luminous solids.

Opposite A view from the exterior through one of the few areas of clear glazing reveals a glimpse of the floating stairs and bridges over the foyer.

Below Top to bottom: Floor plans of the congress hall (on the right) and the auditorium (on the left); cross-section of the auditorium.

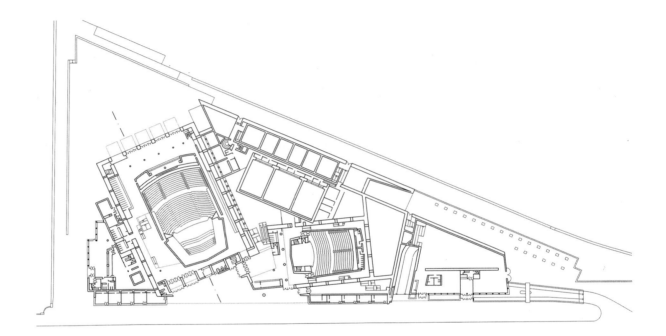

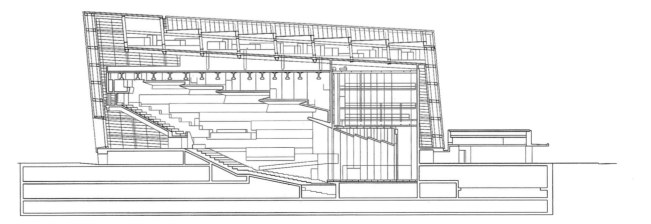

Left Concept sketch – the historical reading room is reinstated as the centrepiece of the museum, now crowned by the glorious glazed roof stretched effortlessly between the drum of the reading room and the classical perimeter wings.

Opposite Long recognized as one of London's most important 'lost' spaces, the courtyard is now an enormously popular public space in the dense urban context of the West End.

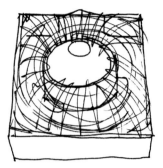

Great Court at the British Museum London, UK 2001

Architects
Foster & Partners

Client
British Museum

Programme
Internal public courtyard
Restored Reading Room
Information centre
Café
Restaurant
Bookshop
Education facilities
New gallery spaces

Location

Built between 1823 and 1847 by the architect Sir Robert Smirke, the British Museum is located in the heart of Bloomsbury, in the centre of London. The museum, built in the neoclassical style, was constructed to house George IV's Royal Library, the donated collections of late eighteenth-century art and antiquities from various connoisseurs, and a remarkable collection of architectural trophies, assembled in the main from Rome, Greece and Asia Minor. By the 1990s the museum was attracting nearly six million visitors a year, more than the Louvre or the Metropolitan Museum of Art.

Site Description

The courtyard at the centre of the British Museum has consistently been regarded as one of London's long-lost spaces. Originally an open garden in Smirke's first plan, soon after the building's completion it became filled by the round reading room of what would become the British Library and its associated shelving systems. With the departure of the British Library, from the museum to St Pancras in 1998, however, the opportunity arose to recapture the courtyard and greatly enhance the museum's facilities and general ease of circulation.

Building Solution

Commissioned to re-establish a public heart in the museum, Foster & Partners immediately set about removing the undistinguished post-war buildings that served as book stacks around the drum of the reading room. While clearing much of this clutter, the architects also restored the listed reading room itself, which would form the focal centre point of the new space and contain an information centre. As completed, the Great Court is entered from the building's principal level, through the museum's grand iconic colonnade, and connects all the surrounding galleries. Within the space of the court itself there are information points, a bookshop and a café. Two broad staircases encircling the reading room lead to two mezzanine levels, ovoid in plan, which in turn provide a gallery for temporary exhibitions and a restaurant above. Below the level of the court are the Sainsbury African Galleries, an education centre with two auditoria, and new facilities for schoolchildren.

Making this whole internal courtyard space possible, and visually providing a newly iconic image for the museum, is the building's glazed roof. For Foster & Partners, the underlying strategy was to produce a canopy that was as delicate and unobtrusive as possible, avoiding any need for supporting columns within the court. Geometrically, the roof also had to negotiate the relationship between the reading room and the surrounding internal façades of the museum, and was further constricted by planning requirements which limited its height relative to existing structures.

The resulting 6,100 square metre (65,655 square foot) roof offers an undulating geometrical form generated by complex mathematical models, which despite its apparent visual consistency and simplicity is made up of over 3,000 triangular glass panels all of which are uniquely sized. Supporting this roof, the structure consists of a fine lattice constructed from purpose-made steel box beams joined at six-way nodes. At its junction with the reading room the roof is supported on a ring of 20 composite steel-and-concrete columns which align with the structural form of the original library's cast-iron frame.

The filigree canopy allows daylight to filter through to illuminate the court, to pass into the reading room and, in very controlled quantities, to also pass into the surrounding galleries. Combining body-tinted glass with a white dot-matrix fritting pattern, the glazing units

Below The structure of the glass roof consists of a geometrically complex fine lattice of purpose-made steel box beams joined at six-way nodes.

Opposite The geometry of the canopy negotiates the differences in height and form between the drum of the reading room (left) and the surrounding internal façades of the museum (right).

achieve a high performance shading coefficient to reduce solar heat gain, yet also transmit a bright and even light across the internal spaces of the court. The glass panels themselves vary in size between 800 millimetres by 1,500 millimetres (31.5 by 59 inches) at their smallest and 2,200 millimetres by 3,300 millimetres (86.5 by 130 inches) for the very largest panels. These panels are also all double-glazed with a 16 millimetre (⅝ inch) air-filled cavity sandwiched between an outer panel of 10 millimetre (⅜ inch) thick tinted and toughened glass and an inner layer comprised of two panes of clear float glass and two clear PVB interlayers. The total thickness of a completed panel is just under 40 millimetres (1.6 inches).

All the Great Court's glazing panels are mechanically restrained by means of stainless-steel bolts and cleats, fixed to the steelwork at 500 millimetre (19.7 inch) intervals around the double glazing units' perimeters. These in turn are manufactured with stepped edges so as to provide the beaming surface for the fixing cleat. Acting as an interface between the supporting steel frame and each of these glass panels is a silicone gasket 15 millimetre (⅝ inch) high. This gasket is not only shaped to cater for the canopy's variable angles, but also to

respond to the combined system's tolerances.

Completed in 2001 the Great Court provided Europe's largest enclosed public space, a glass canopy larger than that of the iron-and-stone dome of St Paul's Cathedral, and an immediately rich and lively cultural quarter.
Beyond the restorative aspect of the architectural brief, however, ultimately it is the overriding sense of transparency and seeming immateriality that animates the whole project. Remarkable because of its light and emptiness, the irony of the Great Court is that in removing a large chunk from the centre of Smirke's old building, clearing away the accretions of 150 years of institutional clutter, the British Museum has discovered a very powerful and compelling sense of focus and identity.

Opposite At its junction with the reading room, the roof is supported on a ring of 20 composite steel-and-concrete columns which align with the structural form of the original library's cast-iron frame.

Left and below The filigree canopy allows daylight to filter through to illuminate the court, and to enter the surrounding galleries.

Opposite As well as being a hugely impressive feat of glass engineering, the Great Court is also Europe's largest enclosed public space.

Below From top to bottom: Site plan of the museum; longitudinal section through the museum; floor plans of the Great Court.

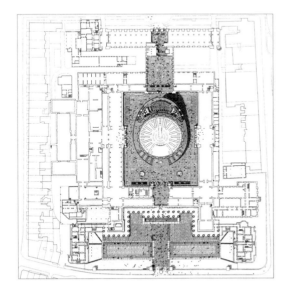

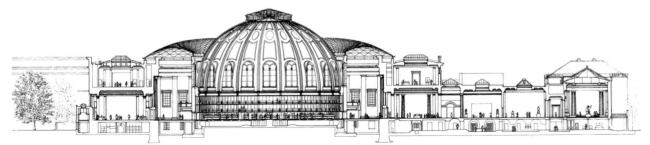

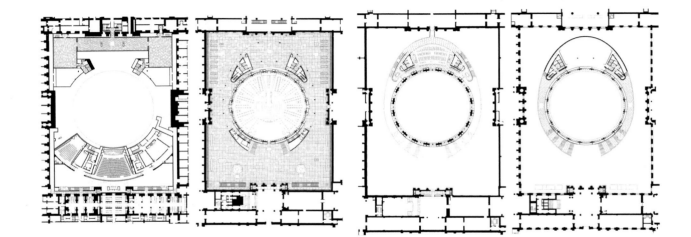

Opposite Concept sketch – despite its outward rectilinear appearance, the key to the design is the iconic Gehry-esque interior atrium where smooth flowing curves and a weightless glass roof transcend the everyday business of banking.

Above left The central courtyard consists of a fully glazed roof, held in place by a delicate steel and glass lattice.

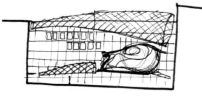

DZ Bank
Berlin, Germany
2001

Architects
Frank Gehry & Partners

Client
DZ Immobilien Management GmbH

Programme
Bank offices
Apartments
Conference centre
Corporate cinema

Location

The DZ Bank is situated in central Berlin on Pariser Platz, opposite the Brandenburg Gate. Built in the nineteenth century predominantly from limestone (like the Brandenburg Gate itself), the platz was originally considered the grandest square in Berlin, and offered an end point to the great urban axis of Unter den Linden. After World War II and the construction of the Berlin Wall, however, the area was laid to waste and became part of the no-man's-land between East and West Berlin. Post reunification, the platz has been gradually rebuilt in an attempt to recapture its former grandeur and central place within the city.

Site Description

The site forms a north-facing urban block, dominated by the new DG Bank headquarters, and flanked by Berlin's new diplomatic quarter, featuring a number of embassies, the Aldlon Hotel, and other blocks of high quality residential apartments and offices. Already existing on the site, opposite the American Embassy, is the studio building of Hitler's architect, Albert Speer. During excavations for the new DZ Bank development, Speer's wartime bunker was also found fully intact under the site. In addition to the preservation of these historical accretions, the rules of reconstruction for the site have stipulated severe restrictions – largely in terms of building height, proportion, and materials (typically stone cladding). Given these many restrictions, the outward reconstruction of the area is characteristically bland, reinstating the original density and street pattern with an architecture that is typically sober, severe and formal.

Building Solution

Situated on the south side of the platz, the site is hemmed in on two sides by the new Akademie der Kunste, by Behnisch & Partners, and the American Embassy, by architects Moore Ruddle Yudell.

For the DZ Bank, the basis of the new scheme has its genesis in Gehry's competition-winning scheme of 1995, which, although at that stage included a museum, was selected also for its adherence to the more commercial aspects of the competition brief.

The mixed-use design solution is essentially pragmatic – providing a simple rectangle, with three sides of banking orientated northwards to the Pariser Platz, and a fourth side offering a residential block facing Behrenstrasse. Despite its outward air of institutional stability, internally the building reveals more of Gehry's signature architecture of sinuous forms and seemingly weightless abstraction. Extending this overriding dichotomy, the building is a reversal of solids and voids: the skin and vestibule areas being all mass, while the interior is a fluid and transparent singular space.

The main elevation is five storeys high, consisting of an ostensibly formal, rationalized, modern architecture with large windows punched deep into the façade, fronted by sheets of glass balustrades enclosing small terraces which overlook the platz and gate. In contrast, the residential façade comprises eight storeys of an undulating concertina surface, which steps back as it rises and houses a combination of private single apartments and larger maisonettes. This residential frontage also has its own entrance, and conceals the rectangular courtyard of the bank beyond, which is arranged right in the heart of the deep plan site. The apartments are segregated from the central courtyard by an ellipsoid atrium, which features a glass wall and two glazed lifts that service the residential spaces above.

The central courtyard is articulated as a scooped out space in which Gehry's

Above left The residential component of the scheme, which houses a combination of single apartments and larger maisonettes, features an undulating surface that steps back as it rises.

Above right The main conference room, an amorphous stainless-steel clad form apparently floating in the atrium, is lined in perforated red oak.

Below left and right At ground-floor level, the spaces are covered with a web-like glass canopy that lets light directly into the heart of the scheme.

spatial pyrotechnics play dramatically against the more sober, European rational plan form. Fully glazed over by a delicate steel and glass lattice, it forms a dramatic barrel-vaulted envelope (curved in two directions) which at roof level appears like the morphed body of a fish, pointed towards the front and with the fan-shaped tail directed towards the rear of the courtyard.

Below the drama of the glazed roof, the atrium is timber clad, six storeys high, with two basement levels below street level and two penthouse levels above the main atrium roof level. The basement houses a lecture theatre and cinema, together with the bank's cafeteria, banqueting suite, and a large foyer space. At ground-floor level, rising over the lower conference centre, the spaces are covered with a warped, web-like glass canopy, which lets light enter directly into the heart of the scheme. From the underside of this curved roof are hung a series of sculptural 'chandeliers', made of fused glass tubes by the artist Nikolas Weinstein, which create opaque cloud forms floating over the conference facility.

Crowning the main space of the atrium is an additional, third, formal element – a free-standing, stainless-steel clad

horse's head-shaped piece, evolved from a flowing but contorted cylinder. The piece is based on an appropriated sculpture study that was used as part of the original architectural competition entry (the final built version is more reminiscent of the upturned hull of a yacht). This houses the main conference room, whose cocooned inner surfaces are lined in perforated red oak for better acoustic performance.

Forming a formal envelope to this sculptural exhibitionism, the DZ Bank's solid and orthodox exterior belies the inner building's complexities and biomorphic forms. As with other Gehry projects, the initial ideas are achieved through a sophisticated design process that is heavily dependent upon both the Catia computer program and a crafted approach to developing working models and drawings. As Gehry himself has commented, the computer is utilized as an 'instrument of translation rather than a generative device, enabling the representation and manipulation of that which cannot otherwise be drawn'. The glass roofs and conference room of the bank demonstrate the extent of this ingenuity, and his ability to maximize the spatial qualities of inner spaces as well anticipating new uses for glass as a curved, and not simply planar, geometry.

In this innovation, the building's roof abandons conventional architecture givens. The main curved glass canopy is made up of a triangulated space frame, comprising solid stainless-steel rods that form six pointed stars screwed into nodal connectors. The complexity of the geometry required that the rods all meet at different angles, so the nodal connectors had to be milled from a 70 millimetre (2.75 inch) thick stainless-steel plate by computer-controlled milling machines. The frame was then clad by 1,500 triangular infills – glazing panels bedded on neoprene gaskets.

Opposite Crowning the central atrium, the form of the main conference room evolved from a flowing, but contorted, cylinder.

Right Detail view of the interior of the conference room – the web-like glazing intrudes on the smooth timber lining to allow natural light in via the glass ceiling of the atrium.

Opposite View of the atrium – Gehry's sculptural use of glass is even more impressive when used, as it is here, as a foil to the orthodox traditional masonry construction employed around the perimeter of the building.

Below Top row: fourth-floor plan; fifth-floor plan; ninth-floor plan. Middle row: Lower ground-floor plan; ground-floor plan; first-floor plan. Bottom row: Cross-section; longitudinal section.

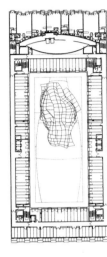
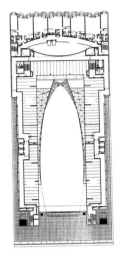
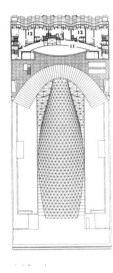
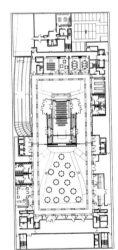
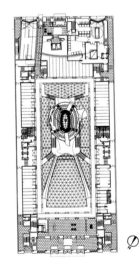
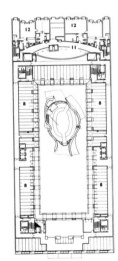
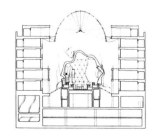
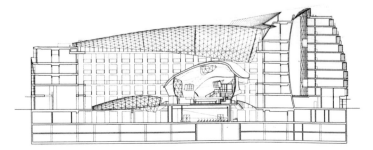

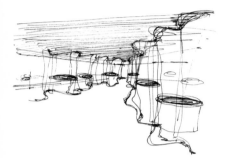

Condé Nast Café
New York, USA
2000

Architects
Frank Gehry & Associates

Client
Condé Nast Publications Inc.

Programme
Employee café
Private dining rooms
Servery

Location

The Condé Nast Café is situated on the fourth floor of the headquarters of Condé Nast Publications House, a 48-storey office tower in Times Square, designed by Fox & Fowle Architects and completed in 1999. Faced with the prospect of moving all of its 20-plus publishing titles to the new headquarters location, the company took the decision to include an in-house dining facility for approximately 260 people that would rival the plethora of diners, cafés and other dining establishments in that area of New York.

Site Description

The site for the café is a rectangular section of a typical (and unremarkable) office floor plate in which the usual paraphernalia of corporate office buildings, including glass curtain walls, lowered ceilings and raised floors, dominate the space. Gehry's brief was to transform this inauspicious tabula rasa into a visionary and inspiring space that would act as the social heart of the organization.

Building Solution

The café has been inserted into a 4.2 metre (14 foot) high space in which Gehry has employed swathes of billowing glass to shape the space both vertically and horizontally. Under a titanium-lined ceiling, clusters of cells (or booths) that accommodate four to six people flow around three sides of the building and into the centre to form islands. Around the periphery where the clusters are tight, the cells are lined with 'Giotto blue' titanium that ebbs and flows in response to the geometry established by the cells. Each cell is defined by curving banquettes, which in the centre are raised up on a plinth of timber-clad concrete and enclosed by extraordinary walls of billowing glass that veil the booths in a seemingly impossible fluidity. Around them a path of ash-veneered plywood rises and falls with the changes in level of the seating areas. To one end of the space a servery continues the sinuous flow of the plan arrangement, while the kitchen and back-of-house facilities are tucked away around the perimeter.

The four private dining rooms are located on the same level as the main dining area and the servery, but are distinct and separate spaces used for special lunch meetings and presentations. Three walls, floors and ceilings of the dining rooms are ash-veneered plywood, while the east wall of each room is composed of overlapping sand-blasted glass panels in which the undulations are magnified by the play of translucent light and shadow.

In a space composed primarily of glass and titanium, an unbearable level of noise might be expected. However, this is successfully overcome through the incorporation of acoustic panelling behind the perforated titanium panelling. At the same time, a sense of traditional café ambience is introduced with the suspended lights (designed by Gehry), yellow laminate tables and quilted banquettes. The dramatic glass walls are composed of immense laminated panels, 22 millimetres (⅞ inch) thick, 3.65 metres (12 feet) high and 1.2 metres (4 feet) wide, each of them different in curvature. Weighing up to 360 kilograms (800 pounds), each panel is fixed top and bottom by 30 centimetre (12 inch) long stainless-steel connectors to a steel frame that is hidden at the top by curved ceiling soffits. Specially designed ball joints in resin grommets prevent the glass from cracking. Modelled by computer, the panels were fabricated by a Californian manufacturer specializing in automotive glass.

The deliberate disruption of anything approaching historical reference or nostalgia for old-fashioned café environments is introduced through the

Right and below Around the seating cells, a path of ash-veneered plywood rises and falls with the changes in level of the seating areas. The glass walls are composed of immense laminated curved panels, each fixed top and bottom by stainless-steel connectors.

Opposite Around the periphery 'Giotto blue' titanium ebbs and flows in response to the geometry established by the seating areas.

use of a single material – glass. This is used in a singularly extraordinary way – more as if it were a pliable fabric than a brittle, transparent material. Instead of the typical use of glass in which windows, portals or panes are used to establish a view from one side to the other, clear glass here is used as a boundary, to delineate one space from another, despite its crystalline transparency. While a sense of openness is deliberately encouraged, and views from one dining area to another are manifest, the billowing layers of glass nonetheless create calming swathes of reflective transparency that engender a sense of privacy and seclusion.

146

Below The four private dining rooms – three walls, floors and ceilings are of ash-veneered plywood, while the remaining wall is constructed from overlapping sand-blasted glass panels.

Opposite Detail view of the sand-blasted glass panels in the private dining rooms – the undulations are magnified by the play of translucent light and shadow.

Following pages Modelled by computer, the glass panels have the effect of challenging our everyday understanding of how glass can, or should, be used.

Left Concept sketch – the concept for the new building proposed a transparent block whose supports are wrapped in glass, and in the process dematerialized.

Opposite View of the western elevation, composed of perforated-steel screens and stairs.

Sendai Médiathèque
Sendai, Japan
2001

Architects
Toyo Ito & Associates

Client
City of Sendai

Programme
Public library
Arts and cultural building
Information centre
Children's library
Multimedia studio
Galleries
Ground-floor public plaza, café and shop

Location
The Médiathèque is situated some 480 kilometres (300 miles) north of Tokyo, Japan, in the prosperous but conservative post-war city of Sendai, a provincial city of one million inhabitants rebuilt after World War II on a spacious grid plan.

Site Description
The site, a former Pachinko gaming parlour, is surrounded by a typical jumble of Japanese contemporary commercial office buildings, apartment blocks, convenience stores and a petrol station. Counteracting this surrounding blandness, the new building offers an architecture of extreme transparency – a transparency generated by a floor-to-ceiling glass envelope. The glass envelope in itself is unremarkable, but the literal transparency of the building's contents, and its openness of public function, is at once reflected and revealed in an intense manner.

This, then, is no ordinary transparency, but is rather something both physical and substantial – the whole interior of the building is captured in one view like an X-ray. Its character is not subtle or ephemeral, but instead offers a permeability which puts all the building's components, and especially the structure, on view. As a glowing 'architectural aquarium' of elements, the building by day, and especially by night, provides a vibrant architectural backdrop for the city.

The Japanese architect Toyo Ito wrote in his *The Garden of Microchips* in 1993: 'The spaces of the contemporary city are characterised by fluidity, multiple layers and phenomenality: these also happen to be the characteristics of microchips.' Central to the evolution of this building are Toyo Ito's own thoughts about contemporary architecture, information and technology. His earlier architectural explorations had progressed from images of sensation and projection to inscription and abstraction.

In this abstraction, Ito leant more towards the deployment of multimedia elements within architecture, to the phenomenology of opacity to transparency, and experiments with pixelization to distort boundaries between the real and the virtual. These ideas reached some kind of zenith at the Sendai Médiathèque, where information technologies appeared to be rendered ubiquitous but invisible.

Ito's concept for the new building proposed a transparent block whose supports were to be wrapped in glass, and in the process dematerialized. Representing an architecture seeking to be liberated from weight, the centre's 'unbearable lightness of being' is founded on three main architectural components: seven floors expressed as flat steel decks; a series of columns composed of bundles of hollow steel tubes on which they are stacked; and an envelope that is wrapped in an enormous and continuous film. The intention behind this three-part system was to present the insides of the building as a beautiful visualization, and to make this content appear more real than the surrounding urban context.

In this pure schematic form, despite its obvious technical innovations, the design also resonated with more traditional Japanese post-and-beam construction, with movable walls and flexible boundaries offered as a contemporary take on the established Japanese emblem of the shoji screen. The clarity of this concept was also heavily indebted to Ito's previous work – notably, the Tower of the Winds, in Yokohama, 1986, his Room of Dreams, from the Victoria and Albert Museum's *Visions of Japan* exhibition, 1991, and to his Inscription project for the University of Paris competition of 1992.

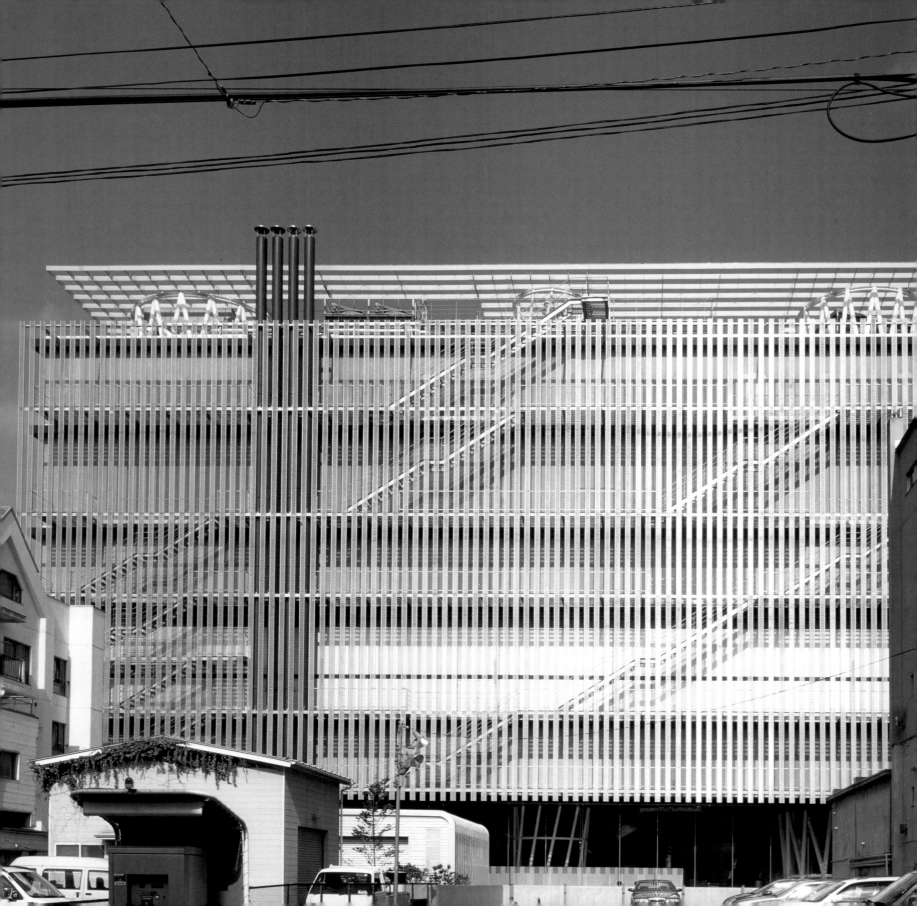

Building Solution

The walls of the Médiathèque enclose a 30 metre (98 foot) high seven-storey building, measuring 50 metres by 50 metres (164 by 164 feet). The composition of this volume is defined by its outer surface – a double layer of glass facing south, curtain walls of glass combined with aluminium and concrete panels to the east and north, and to the west an elevation of perforated-steel screens and stairs. The two glass layers of the southern elevation are separated by 1 metre (3.3 feet) of air space and intermittent glass fins, which stiffen and reinforce the envelope between the two skins. The 19 millimetre (¾ inch) thick outer glass sheet is minimally connected to the inner 10–15 millimetre (⅜–⅝ inch) thick sheet by stainless-steel rods.

So as to prevent excessive overheating, the surface of these glass elevations is fritted with a ceramic patterning silk-screened onto the inner glass surface. The combination of this fritting and the extension of one plane of glass extending beyond another produces a floating quality, as the glass overrides the building envelope but stops short of the roof plane, acting as an extended balustrade to the roof deck and canopy. Additionally, the tight surface quality to the skin of the southern elevation creates a crystalline three-dimensional layering quality in the building's appearance. The space in-between the two glass surfaces functions as an environmental moderator, insulating the inner spaces in winter and venting the overcapacity of heat gained in the height of the summer.

The Médiathèque's overriding celebration of transparency reduces the building to seeming non-existence, reducing architecture to a simple, and apparently immaterial, cube of light. In this reduction, the Médiathèque finds its aesthetic roots not only in the traditional Japanese idea of fragility, translucency and unfixed building enclosures, but also in the western European modern architectural tradition of overcoming architecture's tectonic reality by the pursuit of the transparent and immaterial. The building, in this way, offers both an encapsulated idea and a wrapped box. Ito articulates the varied opacity of the surface, while generating the opportunity for optical flutter and the dissolution of the surface in an endless play of light, darkness, obfuscation, transparency and pattern. This leaves the built effect as ambiguous – opaque and thick with movement and people, the architectural object still maintains a kind of porous neutrality that works both literally and symbolically as the manifestation of the original brief's ambitions.

Below left The two glass layers on the southern elevation are separated by a metre of air space and intermittent glass fins. The outer layer is fritted with a ceramic pattern on the inner surface to prevent solar gain.

Below right The tubular column structures serve as light wells, with rooftop devices to reflect sunlight down the tubes into the building. They also act as vertical connector 'pipelines' for network cables, wiring, elevators and stairways.

Left View of the ground-floor entrance lobby. The highly polished floor surface heightens the effect of light and reflectivity that characterizes the entire scheme.

Below In the typically chaotic Japanese urban context, the Médiathèque offers an architecture of extreme transparency.

Opposite The transparency generated by the floor-to-ceiling glazing becomes even more apparent at night – the building's contents, and its openness of function, are revealed to the public's gaze.

Below Left: Elevation of the Médiathèque; cross-section. Right: Floor plans.

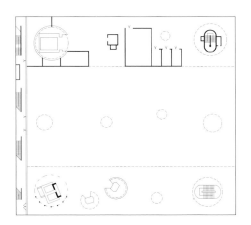

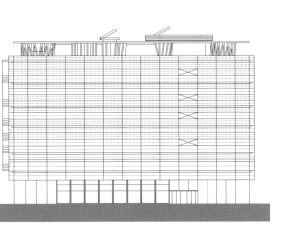

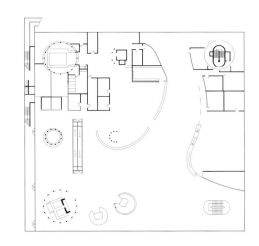

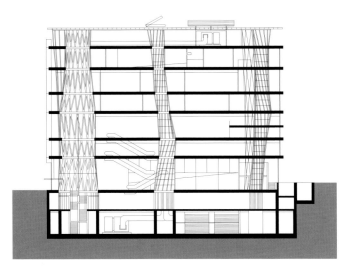

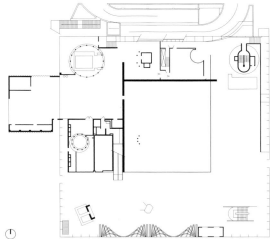

Opposite Concept sketch – the building is organized to evoke the image of 'two jewels in a glass case'.

Right The scale of the glass barrel-vault roof turns the building into a beacon in downtown Philadelphia, and an anchor for the Avenue of the Arts on which it stands.

Kimmel Center for the Performing Arts Philadelphia, USA 2001

Architects
Raphael Viñoly Architects

Client
Regional Performing Arts Center

Programme
Concert hall
Chamber music hall
Proscenium theatre
Black-box theatre
Restaurant
Bar
Back-of-house facilities

Location
The Kimmel Center occupies one full city block of Center City Philadelphia, fronting onto the Avenue of the Arts (formerly Broad Street). The site is located at the corner of Spruce Street, five blocks from the city hall. The centre stands in the heart of the downtown cultural precinct, one block south of the Academy of Music, the Philadelphia Orchestra's long-time home, immediately north of the University of the Arts and four blocks east of the Curtis Institute of Music.

Site Description
The building is organized to evoke the image of 'two jewels in a glass case' – the Verizon Hall for orchestral presentations with its curved cello-shaped interior and the Perelman Theater for chamber music concerts with its polygonal form, are enclosed within a vast perimeter structure. The spaces between and around the two buildings form an indoor plaza, top-lit by day through an immense barrel vaulted roof of folded plate glass. The scale of the structure, in particular the glass barrel-vault, turns the building into a beacon in downtown Philadelphia, and an anchor for the Avenue of the Arts on which it stands. The perimeter envelope of the Kimmel Center is constructed of

glass, steel and brick. The façade along the Avenue of the Arts is largely transparent at street level allowing passers-by to see into the covered public plaza. To maintain the scale of the surrounding residential and cultural buildings, the brick walls rise to approximately the height of the neighbouring University of the Arts.

Building Solution
The Philadelphia Orchestra launched its 'Project for the 21st Century' in 1995 following the campaign to move from its historic but acoustically inadequate home in the much revered Academy of Music, built in an Italianate style in 1857. A year later the Regional Performing Arts Center was set up to create and promote a cultural precinct for Philadelphia that would attract visitors from all over the city and, ambitiously, the world. Based on extensive consultation, a programme was set up to create a new centre for the performing arts that would incorporate a new concert hall for the orchestra.

An architectural competition was organized and architects with proven experience in auditorium design, including Cesar Pelli, Barton Myers and Pei Cobb Freed, were invited to participate. The competition was subsequently won by Raphael Viñoly

with his dramatic vision of a shimmering barrel-vaulted glass roof balanced on steel columns and a sun-drenched atrium enclosing two sculptural auditoria.

The Verizon Hall accommodates 2,500 people in four levels of seating in a sinuous form based on the shape of a cello. The interior surfaces are covered in mahogany, including the ceiling of each tier, reinforcing the image of a finely crafted musical instrument. The entire 29 metre (95 foot) high eight-sided exterior of the hall is clad in horizontal fins of makoré wood, an African cherry, interrupted by circulation balconies cut into the surface.

In contrast to the handcrafted, curving, organic forms of the Verizon Hall, the Perelman Theater is designed as a metal-clad transformable space within the orthogonal form of a 26.5 metre (87 foot) cube. Finished in light woods and warm-coloured fabrics with metallic highlights, the interior of the auditorium complements its soft gold exterior. Designed as an intimate multi-purpose recital hall, the Perelman Theater can also accommodate an audience of 650 for conventional and experimental theatre, music and dance, simultaneously and separately. Its

turntable stage enables the theatre to be transformed from a conventional proscenium-stage configuration to an arena where seating and finishes wrap continuously around the auditorium to complete the horseshoe plan.

The building is surmounted by a transparent, folded-plate Vierendeel trussed glass barrel vault that extends the length of the structure. The 46 metre (151 foot) high vault, spanning 53 metres (174 feet), is constructed from two types of rectangular steel tubes, one 125 by 140 millimetres (5 by 5.5 inches), the other 125 by 115 millimetres (5 by 4.5 inches). The 76 millimetre (3 inch) thick glass panels measure 2 by 1 metres (6.5 by 3.3 feet) each. Slightly tinted low-emissivity glass is used to mitigate heat gain and to act as an ultraviolet shield to preserve the colour and quality of the timber-clad interior walls. The barrel vault terminates at each end in a colossal glass arch using highly transparent glass supported by a gravity-tensioned cable system that supports over 1,000 square metres (10,764 square feet) of optically clear museum glass. Specifically designed as a curtain, as opposed to a mesh, of cables the structure is all but invisible, but can withstand gale force winds by deflecting, like a membrane, 1 metre (3.3

feet) in or out at the centre of its surface. A pair of glass-encased lifts at the front of the centre allow access to a rooftop garden where 16 planter boxes contain large mature trees to create a stunning sky garden overlooking the city.

Without doubt, the identity of the building and its high visibility within the city is a result of the glass barrel-vaulted roof. While it is undoubtedly an engineering tour de force, the simplicity of the form lends the building a grandiloquence of the calibre often associated with the grand engineering schemes of the late nineteenth century, such as the cathedral-scaled railway termini that have captured the imaginations of so many. Like these and other grand public structures of the past century, the roof is used as an urban marker, an iconic image for the city. Again like the railway termini, the plaza becomes a transition space flowing seamlessly between the city and the heart of the complex, used for promenading and for people-watching, with a number of destination alternatives as the end motivation. The result is a luminous structure with a genuine sense of a civic place, an urban ensemble composed primarily of city views, and a building for concert-goers and musicians as well as for Philadelphians.

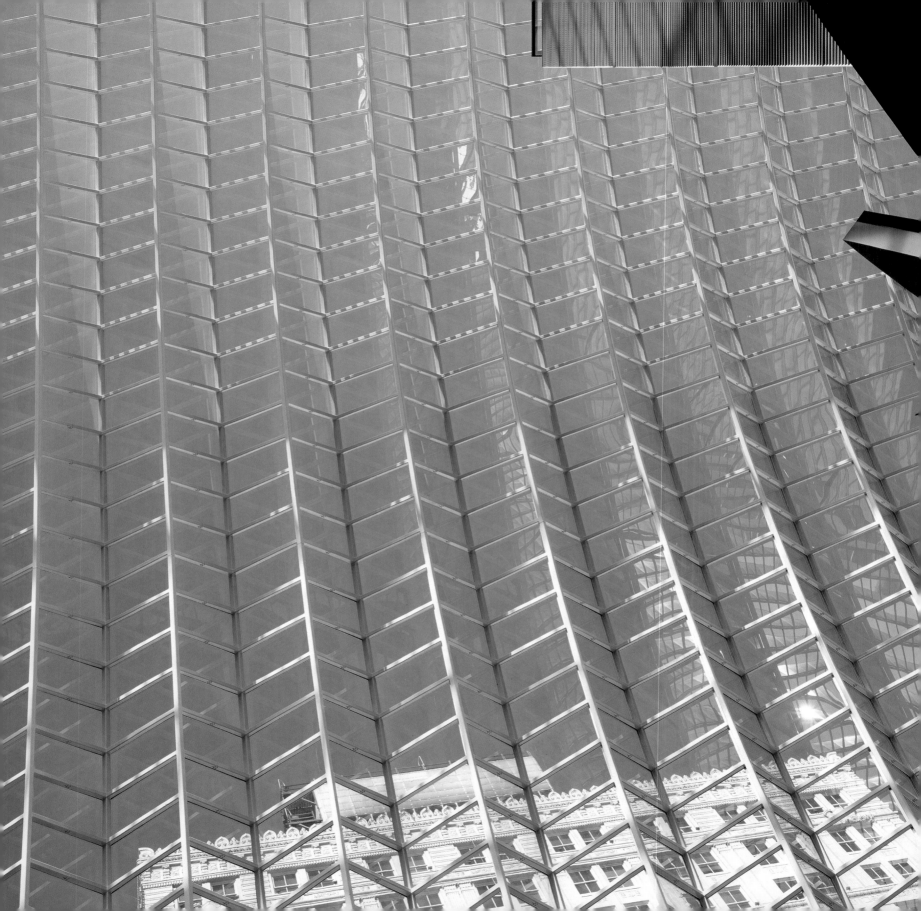

Opposite Tinted glazing mitigates heat gain and acts as an ultraviolet shield to preserve the timber-clad interior walls.

Right The folded plates of the glass barrel vault and neighbouring high-rise towers seen reflected in the flat panes of glass in the arch.

Opposite Like the heroically scaled railway termini of the nineteenth century, the great roof is used as an urban marker, an iconic image for the city.

Left The graceful curve of the glass vault soars over the building.

Left Concept sketch – the house is comprised of two glass pavilions united by white blade walls.

Opposite A series of long, 3 metre (10 foot) high walls extends into the lake and the mature landscaping, while the full-height glazed walls dematerialize the definition between interior and exterior.

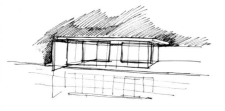

Skywood House
London, UK
2001

Architects
Graham Phillips

Client
Graham Phillips & Diane Phillips

Programme
House
Lake
Bridge
Waterfall and associated landscaping

Location
The house is situated on 1.8 hectares (4.5 acres) of ancient woodland in the Home Counties greenbelt zone west of London, England. With huge mature rhododendrons and in a general state of disrepair, the site came complete with a house suitable for demolition. Greenbelt restrictions and a tree preservation order meant that the new house could contain no more than 250 square metres (2,691 square feet) of floor area and had to fit in with the existing mature tree pattern.

Site Description
The house is comprised of two pavilions united by a 'pinwheel' organization of white blade walls that extend out into the landscape to define the various exterior spaces. The pavilions, one for the four en suite bedrooms and the larger for the living, dining and kitchen spaces (an additional pavilion near the vehicle entrance accommodates the garage and a studio), are rigorously simple and at the same time dramatically elegant in their presentation. The buildings exist in a finely judged counterpoint with the three landscaped spaces – a gravelled entrance court, a lawn overlooked by the bedrooms and the pond that provides the focus for the living room – that define, frame and become an integral part of the architecture.

Building Solution
Designed by the architect-owner Graham Phillips, for himself, his wife and their three children as a permanent home, the original aspiration was to create a 'glass box in the woods'. However, the simplicity of this architectural idea was later expanded to include water as a major element of the design. In addition, the house was designed to dematerialize the relationship between exterior and interior space and in so doing create a series of landscaped rooms that generate a variety of different living experiences.

The carefully managed procession starts at the main gates as one turns the first bend of the black gravel drive. The unexpected vista of the house opens up at the opposite end of the linear lake. One then turns away and travels through mature woods before re-emerging and crossing over a bridge into the main entrance courtyard at the rear of the house. At the bridge one sees the source of the lake water – a simple black obelisk spouting aerated white water. The entrance courtyard forms part of a huge stone plinth on which the house sits, consisting of a perfect square with flush grey limestone paving and an inset black gravel turning circle.

The courtyard is deliberately rendered as a blank space in order to emphasize the purity and simplicity of the form. No garage doors, windows, pipes, gutters or other visual distractions are permitted to impinge on the tranquillity of the arrival ritual. Within this carefully staged sequence, however, the frameless glass entrance door is easily identified. The only architectural element that is specifically expressed in the courtyard is the main chimney riser, which extends beyond the height of the blade walls and the pavilions. This contains all the necessary drainage, ventilation and flue pipes in one integrated unit, while at the same time acting as a signifier for not only the entrance, but also for the symbolic centre of the house – a contemporary interpretation of the 'hearth'.

The plan of the building is based on a classic 'pinwheel' of long, 3 metre (10 foot) high walls that extend well beyond the pavilions into the lake and the mature landscaping, while also defining the pathways. The deceptively simple expression of these walls belies the pre-cast concrete frames that act as vertical cantilevers, and the high-tech insulated render system. The render not only provides high thermal performance and low maintenance but enables the purest

Right View into the living room – the room is anchored by the chimney breast, which integrates television, fireplace and log store in a continuous black slot.

Opposite The original idea of a 'glass box in the woods' is perfectly captured as the pavilion appears to float on the lake. A dividing wall separates the bedroom on the right and the sitting room on the left.

architectural expression without the need for extraneous details such as copings, damp-proof courses or vertical expansion joints.

The two pavilions are comprised of one long wall each of frameless glass and one 3 metre (10 foot) high solid wall and form pure rectangles, adjacent to one another on their short sides but slightly offset in plan to create a juncture at which the entrance and circulation between the two pavilions occur. In the bedroom wing are four double bedrooms each with its own bathroom. The glazing is set out on a 1.8 metre (6 foot) wide module with no openable panes. Instead, ventilation is via the electronically operated rooflights. The bedroom block forms one side of an enclosed walled garden, with a square of lawn set into a black gravel surround.

The glass enclosure that forms the main living area rises slightly higher than the bedroom pavilion, to express the floating steel roof-slab with its 14 metre (46 foot) span and long cantilevers. The double-square floor plate of the main living space, essentially a single open, uncluttered space, extends through the frameless glass to a terrace of the same stone, virtually eliminating the distinction between inside and out. The use of

underfloor heating throughout and the absence of grilles facilitates the entirely flush, seamless detailing. The seating area is defined by a 3.6 metre (12 foot) square of carpet set flush in the honed limestone, continuing the thematic sequence of the landscaped inlays in the courtyard and rear garden. The room is anchored by the chimney breast, which integrates television, fireplace and log store in a continuous black slot.

The kitchen and dining area is equipped with a set of full-height sliding folding partitions and two movable tables which allow a quick change from an open-plan family kitchen arrangement with a long linear bench, to a more formal square dining-table in the centre of the room with the kitchen worktop fully screened from view. Throughout the interior 'aesthetic noise' is carefully edited out. There are no visible switches, plugs or door handles. Every detail is perfectly co-ordinated both technically and geometrically within the 600 by 1,800 millimetre (24 by 72 inch) planning grid to achieve an entirely flush appearance. Even the kitchen taps and the kettle vanish behind sliding panels when not in use.

The living pavilion is focused on the westerly vista over the lake to the island,

which forms a focal point by day and at night when it is dramatically floodlit. The lake has a crisp straight edge on its northern shore, with the neatly mown lawn bringing the edge into sharp focus. The southern shore is more organic in form and this is complemented by the woodland where native plants are encouraged to grow without interference. Within weeks of completion the lake attracted an abundance of wildlife and is now stocked with fish.

This apparently effortlessly simple house belies a feat of complex and sophisticated construction, not to mention a heroic commitment on the part of the architect-owner to invest every detail and every material with the same high degree of care and attention. The glass is undoubtedly the primary material element. However, it is not permitted to dominate the composition. Instead it is employed as an equal partner, along with the smooth white vertical and horizontal surfaces and the carefully managed landscape. In this way, the house celebrates the quintessentially English tradition of the 'picturesque'. It is always appreciated as a part of the natural landscape, whether one's vantage point is within or without. Views of the landscape are framed and edited by the house via the glazing, while

views of the house are just as important and just as managed through the careful and artistic management of the landscape which forms an essential ingredient in the total composition.

Opposite The main living area, essentially a single open space, extends through the frameless glass to a terrace of the same stone as the floor and overlooks the peaceful vista of the carefully manicured lawn and the lake.

Below A slot of glass separates the walls from the ceiling plane, making the living space appear effortlessly light, while a wide slot of louvres in the edges of the roof cantilevers to bring filtered light into the room.

Following pages Views of the house from the lake during the day (left) and night (right).

Left Concept sketch – the primary architectural gesture is the colourful glass cladding which gives the building a highly visible and graphic presence in the city.

Opposite Due to the constricted narrow waterfront site, the floor-plate is extruded upwards into a dramatic 18-storey tower.

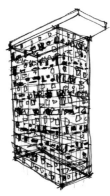

Colorium
Düsseldorf, Germany
2001

Architects
Alsop Architects

Client
Ibing Immobilien Handel GmbH /
Co. Hochhaus KG

Programme
Speculative office building

Location

The Colorium is a speculative office development located in Düsseldorf's dockland area on the Rhine riverfront. The development forms part of the masterplan to rejuvenate this dilapidated part of the city and contributes to its transformation into the Mediahafen (or Media Harbour), where a new generation of electronics entrepreneurs are establishing Düsseldorf as Germany's premier city of communication. The Colorium sits alongside a number of buildings designed by internationally celebrated architects such as Frank Gehry, Steven Holl, David Chipperfield and Fumihiko Maki on the Speditionsstrasse peninsula.

Site Description

The site, formerly the location of a waterfront silo, is constricted into a long narrow rectangle. As a result, the narrow floor plate is extruded upwards into a dramatic 18-storey, 62 metre (203 foot) high tower in order to generate as much office space as possible within the constraints of the site, the tight budget and planning regulations.

Building Solution

The plan layout and structure of the Colorium are conventional – a concrete frame with circular perimeter columns, braced by an offset core positioned along the south side. Standard flexible partitions divide the floors into a range of lettable spaces for commercial tenants. Despite the prosaic nature of the brief, architectural and technical sophistication are introduced in a dramatic gesture, concentrated in the cladding to give the building a highly visible and graphic presence in the city. The orthodox curtain-wall system employs 17 distinct types of glass panels, windows and spandrels which are mounted in prefabricated aluminium frames. The panels are silk-screen printed with 30 colours in a pattern devised to disrupt the visual impact of the scale and shape of what is, in effect, a conventional tower block. This mechanized 'serigraphic' printing process uses viscous inks forced through a nylon screen. The fast production runs and extremely high definition and colour quality result in a crisp and perfectly executed design that is capable of being repeated across the entire façade.

Colours are restricted in the double-glazed window infill panels where the low-emissivity coatings are decorated with a silk-screen matrix that renders the blocks of colour less opaque, therefore encouraging views out across the harbour and the city. The views, however, are edited by these blocks of colour, which reframe and disrupt, concentrating the gaze through and around the graphic composition. The building is naturally ventilated – every other patterned pane is openable, although in a manner that fails to disrupt the overall impression of a continuous graphic across the surface of the building. Similarly, the horizontal elements of the structure are emphasized with a composition of opaque glass panels that form subtle bands of solid and patterned colour running horizontally across the building. Again, at first glance, the regular rhythm of the spandrels fails to make an impression, encouraging the sense of a graphic design that uses the entire façade as an even canvas.

The building terminates in a red light-box that cantilevers on steel truss-frames over the wharf frontage, concealing the rooftop plant. Originally intended to accommodate a restaurant and penthouse with commanding views over the city, this element nonetheless succeeds in engaging the building with its context, where it is reflected in the water and, at night, visible across the city. The Colorium is unapologetic about its status as a decorated box. In

Right Views over the harbour and the city are edited by the blocks of colour that reframe and disrupt, concentrating the gaze through and around the graphic composition.

Opposite The building terminates in a red light-box that cantilevers on steel truss-frames over the wharf frontage.

precisely and functionally answering the demands imposed by the client's brief, it stands proudly, even brashly, among its stately, sometimes reticent neighbours, acting as a symbol for the aspirations of Düsseldorf's new media precinct.

The achievement of this project is the utilization of established, even prosaic, technologies to create a building that is more than the sum of its parts. The ability of the signage industry to generate and apply thin layers of graphic complexity has been co-opted here on a scale that transcends the everyday manipulation of advertising and information. Combined with the sophistication of modern glass curtain wall building technology, in which Germany is a recognized leader, the Colorium illustrates the rich and exciting possibilities for the future of glass façade treatments.

Below and opposite The curtain wall system employs 17 distinct types of glass panels, windows and spandrels, silk-screen-printed with 30 colours in a pattern devised to disrupt the visual impact of the scale and shape of the building.

Following pages The coloured glass was created using a mechanized printing process resulting in a high-definition colour quality.

Opposite The horizontal elements of the structure are emphasized with a composition of opaque glass panels that form subtle bands of solid and patterned colour running across the façades.

Below Left top to bottom: Site plan of Colorium; typical office-level floor plan; ground-floor plan. Right: Section of the tower.

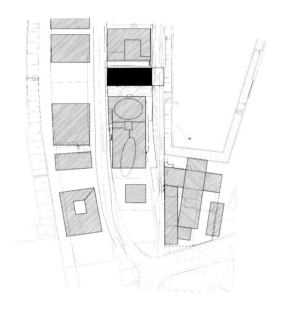

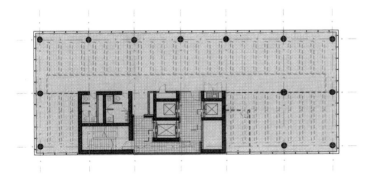

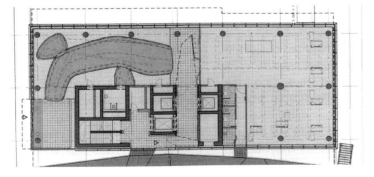

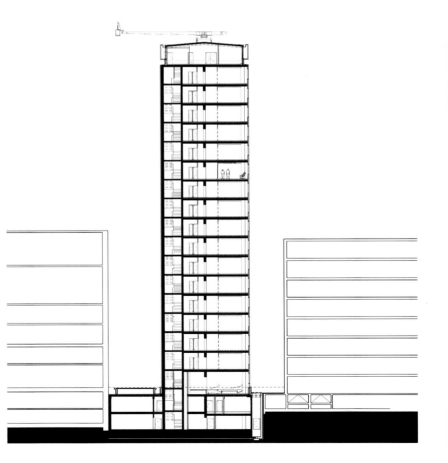

Left Concept sketch – the glass façade expresses the process of communicating with local people through a building that is transparent, open and inviting.

Opposite The elevations are treated as a continuous but layered skin, wrapping around and connecting all parts of the building.

City Hall
Alphen aan den Rijn, The Netherlands
2002

Architects
Erick van Egeraat Associated
Architects

Client
Municipality of Alphen aan den Rijn

Programme
City hall
Services department
Administrative facility

Location
Located in the centre of the Netherlands, Alphen aan den Rijn is a city of modest size, and home to some 70,000 people. However, it has major ambitions, with plans for the redevelopment of the entire city centre. Erick van Egeraat's city hall forms the centrepiece of the masterplan and is destined to set the tone for future developments within the city.

Site Description
The building is located between a civic plaza to the south and a smaller-scale residential district to the north. The city hall itself is a free-form curvilinear building occupying the south end of the site, while at the north end is a lower office block with a large exhibition and conference hall between the two.

Building Solution
The city council sought to represent their approach to administration and the process of communicating with local people through a building that is transparent, open and inviting. The building's appearance relates directly to this ambition and is expressed primarily through the transparent glass façade. The choice of light and natural materials for the interior also reinforces the building's public character of the institution and is intended to encourage visitors and citizens to participate in public life.

The council felt that an innovative architectural statement was appropriate to express their remit, which is reflected in a free-form, curving exterior. The overall form was defined in such a way that it relates to, and reunites, the scale differences of the immediate urban context. On one side the building is higher to respond to the city scale of the Raoul Wallenberg Square, while on the remaining sides the building is more modest in scale, where it faces the residential area. The main entrance is located on the south-east corner, addressing the Stadhuisplein. This opens into a spacious reception area with a broad flight of stairs leading to the assembly chamber above, which projects over the entrance to express its accessibility to the public.

The elevations are treated as a continuous but layered skin, wrapping around and connecting the three parts of the building, comprised of the city hall, the services department and administration facilities. The various layers slide over one another, revealing a surface that is appropriate for the function it covers, and allowing the different parts of the complex to express their own individuality. The main volume of the city hall features transparent elevations with an enclosed atrium behind. The lower volume, containing the services department and administrative area, is predominantly constructed of masonry and is substantial in character, although incorporating a degree of transparency to allow for natural day-lighting and views out of the building.

The double-curved tempered-glass panels that characterize the outward appearance of the building are held in place top and bottom in stainless-steel U-profile sections. The photographically applied leaf-print pattern that covers the entire surface of the building fits together like a puzzle. Inside and out, the decorative effect also provides solar control and a measure of privacy for the building's users. The pattern appears more dense on those elevations exposed to direct sunlight, casting cool shadows reminiscent of a leafy forest. The pattern thins out again where solar gain and glare are less of an issue.

By changing its appearance, much like a chameleon responds intuitively to its environment, the city hall responds to both its programmatic and spatial requirements, as well as sensitively

reacting to the urban nuances of its context. Without succumbing to the historically monumental image of the city hall, the building is nonetheless an iconic gesture and a radical new presence in the city. It is at once an open, inviting and accessible institution, reflecting the image of this growing community.

Below Various layers of the façade slide over one another, revealing surfaces that are appropriate to the function they cover, thereby allowing different parts of the complex to express their own individuality.

Opposite The main entrance opens into a spacious reception area with a broad flight of stairs leading to the assembly chamber above, which projects over the entrance to express its accessibility to the public.

Below and opposite The double-curved tempered-glass panels are covered in a leaf pattern that provides solar control as well as a measure of privacy for the building's users.

Opposite Interior view of the building showing the high degree of natural day-lighting.

Below Ground-floor plan and longitudinal section.

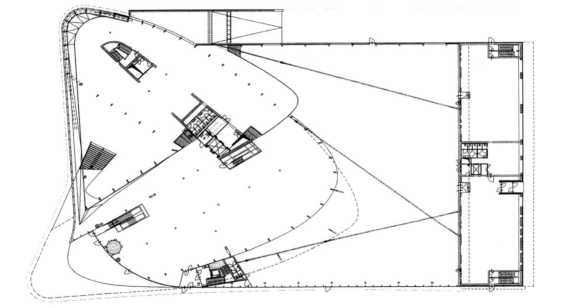

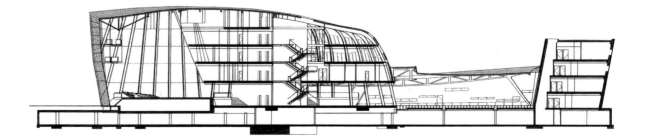

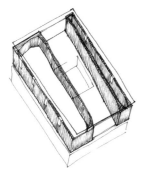

Laminata House
Leerdam,
The Netherlands
2002

Architects
Kruunenberg Van der Erve Architects

Client
Leerdam Housing Association
(GWL Koopwoningen)

Programme
Glass house for an artist

Location
The site is a single residential plot near the town of Leerdam, the home of the glass industry in the Netherlands. The building was the result of an architectural competition run by the local housing foundation, GWL Koopwoningen, to mark the 40th anniversary of the Leerdam Housing Corporation.

Site Description
The house covers a rectangular plot of 500 square metres (5,382 square feet). The building is principally expressed as a single-storey flat-roofed house. On plan it is split into two parts longitudinally; the larger portion accommodates the main house with two double bedrooms, shared bathroom and study. The smaller portion accommodates a WC and entrance hall. Between the two wings is an open-plan living and dining space with adjacent terrace, and an open double-height entry courtyard that descends to a basement level housing a garage and studio space.

Building Solution
The Laminata House is a unique architectural solution that exploits the use of glass for its main façades, but not as flat-sheet or double-glazed units in the more typical manner. Rather, the walls and indeed the entire structure are composed purely of glass. It is a bold experiment that employs glass sheets structurally, while at the same time responding to the privacy and security requirements of the inhabitants.

The house is comprised of individual layers of 1 centimetre (⅜ inch) thick laminated glass, stacked vertically as 10,000 separate sheets that are cut individually and glued on site with a silicon-based sealant, to provide solid glass forms from which the internal spaces are carved out. The width of the resulting walls varies from 20 centimetres (8 inches) to 2 metres (6.5 feet). The curving path taken by the 'knife' with which the glass is carved is best seen in the main hallway that runs the entire north–south length of the house from the entrance to the main living areas. Here the glass ebbs and flows in a finely honed sculptural mass, the exposed ends of the sheets of glass creating an unexpectedly rich pattern that ripples across the surface of the walls, enhanced by the play of light and shadow. The variable light traversing the uneven thickness of the walls creates a striking effect, passing from the dense protective opacity of the thickest walls to end in the limpid transparency of the thinnest plates.

The lengthy four-and-a-half year research, development and construction programme was partly caused by the difficulty in finding a suitable glue with which to bond the sheets of glass. However, a revolutionary solution was developed in order to ensure that the glue used is UV-resistant and permanently flexible while accommodating the expansion and fragility of the glass. Thus there is a certain amount of structural movement preserved between each sheet of glass in order to provide flexibility in the whole. As for strength, although a single sheet can easily be shattered by a hammer, taken together the laminated glass is stronger than concrete. The experimental solution was the outcome of a unique collaboration between the architects, the Netherlands Institute for Applied Science (TNO) based in Delft (responsible for the preliminary research exercise) and the glass company Saint Gobain (who carried out the glass fabrication) and Den Braven Sealants, based at Oosterhout.

The building is located on a concrete slab, and served by underfloor heating and an electrical conduit system. The inherent thickness of the walls absorbs heat gain and dissipates it without transferring it to the interior, and thus

Right 10,000 separate sheets of glass were cut individually and glued on site. The exposed ends of the glass create an unexpectedly rich pattern that ripples across the surface of the walls.

Opposite The unique building solution exploits glass for the entire structure – individual layers of 1 centimetre (⅜ inch) thick laminated glass are stacked vertically to create solid glass forms. Used in this way, the glass loses its fragility, becoming weighty and acquiring a mass and volume more commonly associated with masonry.

eliminates heat fluctuations and the need for cooling in the summer months. However, it was recognized that the same walls presented a particular challenge due to the inability to create penetrations for service cabling.

The result is an astonishing feat and, unlike other glass buildings, is unique in its treatment of light and its 'ice-like' volumetric mass. Unlike previous experimental essays in the use of glass as an architectural material, in which it is employed primarily for its apparent weightlessness and transparency, Gerard Kruunenberg and Paul Van der Erve have contrived to renew the experiential properties of the material. Here, glass loses its fragility, becoming weighty and acquiring mass and volume. The result totally redefines the use of glass as a building material, and as a result represents an architectural revolution.

Opposite left and right In the hallway (right) the glass ebbs and flows in a finely honed sculptural mass.

Left The 'ice-like' shards of the cut ends of the glass sheets provide a startlingly original surface on which to hang a portrait.

Opposite Interior view showing the varying degrees of transparency and light quality created by the glass walls.

Below Ground-floor plan and cross-section of the glass house.

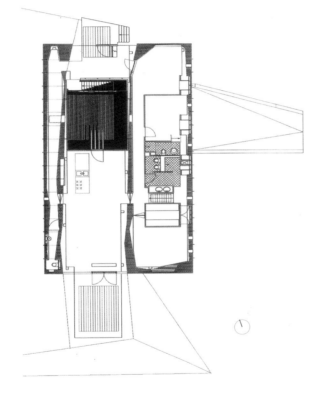

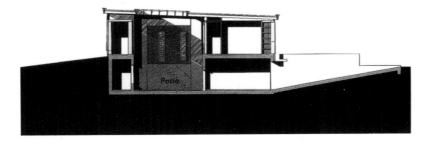

Left Concept sketch – the building is arranged as an inflected box, with a curved face masking the principal entry hall.

Opposite The structure superficially appears as an industrial shed – an orthogonal silhouette punctured by just a few openings that appear as warehouse doors. However, the sweep of glass panels belies its true nature as an undeniably sophisticated structure.

Laban Dance Centre
London, UK
2003

Architects
Herzog & de Meuron

Client
Laban Centre

Programme
Theatre
Production facilities
Studio theatre
Library
Health centre
Cafeteria
Dance studios
Administration

Location

The Laban Centre is situated in Deptford, south-east London, a largely industrial suburb immediately west of Greenwich. Traditionally regarded over the last century as the epicentre of south-east London's industrial wasteland, the area has more recently been highlighted for wholesale gentrification, precipitated by the extension of London's Jubilee Line underground network, and the resulting connectivity of Deptford to the office towers of Canary Wharf on the north side of the Thames, and the City and the West End of London.

Site Description

The site itself was a former rubbish dump located above a soft curve of Deptford Creek (a tidal tributary of the Thames separating Deptford from Greenwich) and is surrounded by a hodgepodge of offices, shops and housing developments, together with the more romantic outlines of barges and tugboats stranded at low tide in the adjacent creek. Dictating the gentle curve of the resulting building's westerly elevation is the nearby St Paul's Church (1730), designed by the British baroque architect Thomas Archer, while facing east the centre also had to accommodate views of Greenwich's

famous eighteenth-century sailing ship, the *Cutty Sark*, which is permanently moored alongside the observatory.

Building Solution

The structure superficially appears as just another industrial shed – an orthogonal silhouette punctured by just a few openings that appear as warehouse doors. But the closer one gets to the building, the more this image of a generic industrial vernacular is dissolved. Rather than regulated 90-degree angles, the centre actually represents an inflected box, with a curved face masking the principal entry hall. Approached across a grassed landscape featuring trapezoid mounds of recycled earth (designed by Swiss landscape architects Vogt Landschaftarchitekten), kaleidoscopic reflections of the building's immediate context animate the concave elevation's sweep of glass panels. This exterior skin hovers just above the ground plane, accentuating the centre's visual lightness, and separating this surface from the building's concrete structure. In this way the centre appears to float. Air can circulate within a gap between the building's outer polycarbonate skin and its taut inner membrane of washed-out glass, creating a thermal and acoustic buffer zone.

Inside, the centre of Laban is made up of a network of corridors, or 'streets', and chambers on two full storeys with a mezzanine in-between. Public spaces, such as the café and library are located next to the building's entrance, overlooking the muddy banks of Deptford Creek. The entry-hall floor splits around a dramatic black lacquered concrete spiral stair, one side of which descends down into the café and administrative offices, while the other ramps up to the dancers' studios. At the heart of the building is an enclosed 300-seat performance space, entirely clad in birch as a kind of shed within a shed, that rises up through the building, reaching its zenith with the stage's fly-tower just beneath the building's barely perceptible pitched roof.

More than its internal configuration, however, ultimately it is Laban's display of light and colour that really distinguishes the architecture. The composition of polycarbonate and glass provides an extraordinarily varied set of interior conditions – not just shifting colours, but also opaque and translucent surfaces. All the windows that puncture the polycarbonate are made from mirrored glass, so that during the day, in their reflectivity, these apertures obscure views of the interior

Below and opposite Night and daytime views – the windows that puncture the polycarbonate are made from mirrored glass, so that during the day they obscure views of the interior from passers-by, while at night the back-lit glass becomes transparent so that moving shadows are projected onto the polycarbonate façade.

Following pages During the day the polycarbonate surface of the walls provides an ever-changing coloured backdrop for the dancers' studios.

from passers-by. Conversely, daylight passing through the polycarbonate surface provides an ever-changing coloured backdrop to the translucent glazed walls of the dance studios. At night, however, this whole process is reversed, with the back-lit glass becoming transparent, so that the dancers' moving shadows are projected onto the polycarbonate façade of the building.

This treatment of light is combined with a highly original use of colour. Working with English artist Michael Craig Martin, Herzog & de Meuron have devised a limited palette of slightly altering colours – blue becomes turquoise, green becomes lime – with bold colours used internally to pick out walls and services, and just three colours (turquoise, green and magenta) used on the outside of the building. The colour is added during extrusion to the inner leaf of the polycarbonate (hence the building's shimmering illusion) and projects its faint tone inside onto the centre's white walls.

Through this treatment of light and colour, Laban really offers something quite radical. Within the history of glass in modern architecture it represents a clear break from the old Miesian ideal – which originated with his Kaistrasse

skyscraper project and then became a paradigm of domestic living with the Farnsworth House – of the all-glass building as being transparent and in effect colourless. The virtue of this model was one of absence – everything had been removed, with even the obvious materiality of the glass denied by an overriding sense of the immaterial. What Herzog & de Meuron seem to have introduced to this ideal is the idea of presence – of colour, shadow and even opacity. And in the process they have reinvented the apparently sacrosanct image of the glass box. That they have done this not with a huge budget and a shimmering headquarters for a major corporation, but for £13 million and a dance studio in south-east London, is all the more impressive.

Opposite The entrance hall splits around a dramatic black lacquered concrete spiral stair, one side of which descends down into the café and administrative offices, while the other ramps up to the dancers' studios.

Below left and right The use of glass and manipulation of light is integral to the concept of the building. The composition of polycarbonate and glass provides an extraordinarily varied set of shifting colours in the opaque and translucent surfaces.

Opposite The industrial and maritime setting of Deptford provides a seemingly unlikely location for a dance centre. Public spaces, including the café and library, overlook the muddy banks of Deptford Creek.

Below Top to bottom: Lower-floor plan showing the dance theatre within the centre and surrounding dance studios; upper-floor plan.

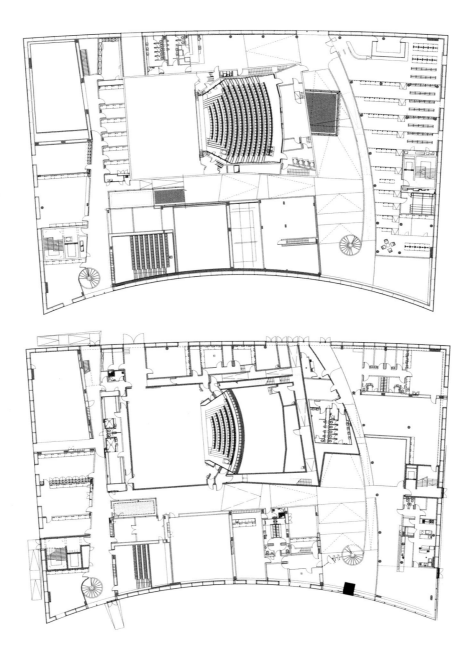

30 St Mary Axe
London, UK
2004

Architects
Foster & Partners

Client
Swiss Reinsurance Company

Programme
Office space
Kitchen facilities
Private dining rooms
Bar
Restaurant

Location
30 St Mary Axe is located within the centre of a 56 hectare (1.4 acre) freehold site in the heart of London's insurance district. Bounded by St Mary Axe, Bury Street, Bury Court and Browns Buildings, the site contains the severely damaged remains of the listed former Baltic Exchange. To the north is the Grade II listed building at 38–40 St Mary Axe and to the east lies Holland House, a similarly Grade II listed building.

Site Description
The site itself is situated within the City of London, the capital's financial district, and unusually, despite its central location, is not bound by many of the planning restrictions that affect much new building in the City. This freedom stems largely from the fact that the site lies east of the cluster of high buildings grouped around Tower 42 (Richard Seifert's 18 metre/60 foot tower for the National Westminster Bank) and so is free of the height constraints imposed on the City by the strategic view corridors of St Paul's Cathedral and the Monument. In its proximity to this post-war financial centre, the site also falls outside the City's conservation area, and the fact that its footprint represents an island, with continuous pedestrian routes around it and with no underground tunnels beneath, meant that it offered its architects the opportunity for much greater freedom of expression.

Building Solution
The building itself, a 40-storey skyscraper, has been dubbed London's first ecological skyscraper by its architects, Foster & Partners. Designed around a pine-cone design (as promoted by its architects) and referred to as 'the gherkin' (by the public), the tower forms an instantly recognizable addition to London's skyline, while embodying a highly progressive environmental strategy, with its aerodynamic shape maximizing the amount of natural lighting and ventilation and in the process reducing the building's energy consumption.

The building was designed for Swiss Re, one of the world's leading reinsurance companies, and brings together all the company's London-based staff in a single headquarters. Inside, 40,000 square metres (430,500 square feet) of its interior layout is taken up by office space, while its ground floor is given over entirely to the public, with shops and cafés spilling out onto the adjoining plaza. Higher up, above the office spaces, level 38 provides kitchen facilities and private dining rooms, level 39 a restaurant, and the top floor, level 40, a bar, all of which enjoy panoramic 360-degree views over London.

The form of the building was generated through a series of complex fluid dynamic studies of the local environmental conditions, which suggested a strategy for integrating the building within its site, and allowing it to use natural forces of ventilation. The resulting 180 metre (590 foot) tall tower breaks with the conventions of traditional box-like office buildings in being built around a circular plan, tapered at the base and the crown to improve connections to the surrounding streets and allow the maximum amount of daylight at plaza level.

Outside, the surface articulation of the tower explores a series of progressive curves, developed with the aid of parametric computer-modelling techniques. Taking its cue from many forms that recur in nature, the building is structured around a spiral and, again like the surface of a pine cone or other natural precedents, is able to open and close in response to changes in the weather. Framing these spirals, the building is structured via a sequence of diagonal steel braces which, by virtue of their triangulated form, are inherently

Top The cladding consists of flat triangular and diamond-shaped glass panels which are differently shaped at each floor.

Bottom View of the entrance, where the glazing is stripped away to reveal the scale of the main structural elements.

Opposite View of the double-height entrance lobby.

strong and efficient, and frees up the interior spaces to be highly flexible and column-free.

The exterior cladding consists of 5,500 flat triangular and diamond-shaped glass panels which are differently shaped at each floor. The glazing of the office areas consists of a double-glazed outer layer and a single-glazed inner screen that sandwich a central ventilated cavity which accommodates the building's solar-control blinds. These cavities also act as buffer zones to reduce the need for additional heating and cooling, and are ventilated by exhaust air which is drawn in from the offices. The glazing to the light wells that spiral up the tower is made up of openable double-glazed panels with a combined grey-tinted glass and high-performance coating that effectively reduces solar gain.

In its fusion of the idea of gardens and the commitment to high-rise, 30 St Mary Axe in many ways resurrects the recurring images of organicism and architecture of the Archigram group in the 1960s, and their various tower proposals. For Norman Foster, the tower is more readily explained as an extension of the work his office did in the 1980s on the Climatroffice project, with the American architect and innovator Buckminster Fuller. Either way, the building provides a striking new silhouette on London's skyline while satisfying many of the opportunities for innovation afforded by its site.

Below left and right Atria between the radiating fingers of each floor link together vertically to form a series of informal break-out spaces that spiral up the building.

Opposite At the top of the building – London's highest occupied floor – a restaurant and private bar offers a spectacular 360-degree panorama across the capital.

Opposite 30 St Mary Axe is London's first ecological tall building and an instantly recognizable addition to the city's skyline.

Below Left: Elevation. Right: Typical office-floor plan illustrating the central service and structural core surrounded by the usable fingers of floor area (in black), interspersed with voids at the perimeter.

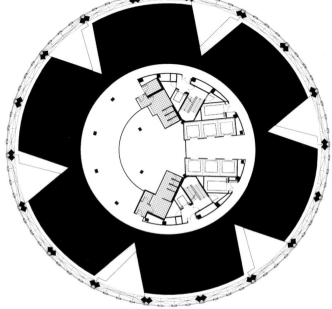

Left Concept sketch – the constraints posed by two adjacent protected structures and the incorporation of Eisernes Haus into the Kunsthaus programme contributed in no small way to the unique form of the building.

Right A matrix of doughnut-shaped fluorescent lights stretches across the eastern surface of the shell, and can be programmed to display images, films and animations in low resolution.

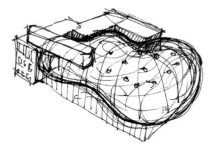

The Kunsthaus
Graz, Austria
2004

Architects
Spacelab Cook
Fournier

Client
City of Graz/Kunsthaus Graz AG

Programme
Museum of modern and
contemporary art
Reading and media lounge
Performance space
Exhibition spaces
Shop
Café
Bar
Viewing pavilion

Location
The Kunsthaus (Museum of Art) is situated in the heart of the Austrian city of Graz on the western bank of the river Mur in the baroque quarter of Murvorstadt. The Kunsthaus stands at the corner of Südtirolerplatz and the Lendkai in the old town, and opposite the Uhrturm (clock tower), a prominent city landmark. The city of Graz intends the new museum to act as an interface between the past and the future and as a startling new icon for the city. The integration of additional cultural institutions into the baroque buildings adjacent to the Kunsthaus further reinforces the intensity of the city's new cultural cluster.

Site Description
The site for the Kunsthaus was created following the demolition of several houses between Lendkai and Mariahhilferstrasse, opening up a gap in the fabric of the city. Due to the constraints posed by two adjacent protected baroque structures and the incorporation of another listed structure (Eisernes Haus) into the Kunsthaus programme, the resulting size and geometry of the site were irregular and demanding, and contributed in no small way to the unique form of the building.

Building Solution
For decades, Graz had lacked a gallery dedicated to the display of contemporary art. This deficit, however, had certain advantages. It forced exhibition organizers to find temporary solutions, for example in warehouses, castles and other locations throughout the city. Often these changing and sometimes challenging conditions resulted in memorable and successful exhibitions, imbued with the character of an environment that was not 'made to measure'. While designed and built as a bespoke art space, the Kunsthaus nonetheless continues the tradition of Graz's cultural scene. The shape and nature of the interior spaces, defined by the exterior form, are anything but the typical orthogonal white spaces of many contemporary art galleries.

The process of developing the brief for the Kunsthaus began with the preparation of a detailed museological programme commissioned by the city of Graz. The programme placed equal emphasis on the multidisciplinary demands of contemporary art, the communication of art and culture to the public, and the intensification of a discussion of new media, without the necessity of providing infrastructure for the storage and conservation of a permanent collection. In so doing, the building attempts to mediate between the need to stand out as an urban-scale object in its own right, and unobtrusively and efficiently service the works of art it shelters.

The programmatic arrangement consists firstly of an open ground floor that acts as a meeting place for artists and art enthusiasts. With two main entrances, one from the Lendkai and the other from Südtirolerplatz, the space includes information, communication and entertainment facilities, complete with bookshop, museum store, café and multi-purpose event space. From the ground floor, a 30 metre (98 foot) long travelator, known as 'the pin', takes visitors up to the 1,800 square metre (19,375 square foot) main gallery on the first floor and the 'media platform' equipped with mobile projection cells, interactive communication stations and communication area.

The main gallery sits beneath the structural shell, which soars to 8 metres (26 feet) at its highest point. The shell is punctuated by 'light 'nozzles' equipped with adjustable daylight and artificial light sources, the cones of the nozzles contributing to the distinctive appearance of the internal and external

skin. A glazed link connects the ground and first floors to the cultural facilities of the adjoining Eisernes Haus (Iron House), a well-known icon in Murvorstadt constructed in 1848. From the first floor, visitors leave the 'bubble' and enter a horizontal glass structure called 'the needle' where a bar and expansive views over Graz create an atmosphere of relaxation and reflection.

The demanding complexity of the museum programme, which included the maintenance of constant temperature and humidity levels, natural and artificial light levels, and highly technical conservation and security systems, could not be met simply by stretching a light, transparent skin over the frame of the building, although this was, by implication, the desired outcome as expressed in the competition scheme. In the finished building, the multilayered skin incorporates all the technical elements required by a contemporary museum, including sprinkler systems, insulation, air-conditioning, electrical and media wiring, mounting supports for lights and artworks, as well as the primary steel and concrete structure. On the interior, an inner skin of triangular panels of finely woven grey wire cloth acts as a barely present spatial enclosure and hanging

system, through which the exterior skin is partly visible.

Beyond the architectural, structural and technical necessities, the task of implying the transparent nature of the building was taken over by a large-scale media façade incorporated into the skin, 'illuminating' the contents by broadcasting them to the city. The extraordinary outer hull of the Kunsthaus is made not from glass but from an acrylic material with, at least superficially, similar properties to glass, including transparency, reflectivity and an apparent fragility, lending the building the quality of a delicate vessel. While the acrylic appears at first glance to be a seamless moulded 'blanket' covering the entire structure, it is, in fact, a veneer. It does not perform any structural function (other than supporting itself), nor any environmental function, such as weatherproofing (except in the case of the funnels which admit natural light). Nor, in the main, does it act as a visual portal from the interior to the exterior (or vice versa) as practical requirements for the exhibitions require largely impermeable wall surfaces.

In the case of the Kunsthaus, the skin acts primarily as a sign, an image and a work of art in its own right – a sign for the

city, for the museum, for the exhibitions and, most importantly, as a tool for media and light artists. The matrix of 930 doughnut-shaped fluorescent lights stretched across the eastern surface of the shell (referred to as 'BIX') is capable of being programmed to display images, films and animations in low resolution. By regulating the brightness of each individual light from 0–100 per cent in 1/20th of a second using special software and hardware, the Kunsthaus is able to radically alter its appearance from one second to the next. While capable of being used as a conventional advertising tool, the BIX installation is seen primarily as an 'experimental field' on which artists can demonstrate cultural and artistic ideas that would ordinarily be banned from the surfaces of commercially used architectural façades.

Left An inner skin of triangular panels of finely woven grey wire cloth acts as a barely present spatial enclosure and hanging system.

Right At the top of the building, the shell is punctuated by 'light nozzles' that contribute to the distinctive appearance of the external skin.

Opposite The new museum acts as an interface between the past and the future, and as a startling new icon for the city.

Below left and right The outer hull of the Kunsthaus is made from an acrylic material with similar properties to glass, lending the building a quality of unexpected fragility.

Opposite The main ground-floor entrance space includes information, communication and entertainment facilities, complete with bookshop, museum store and café.

Below Left top to bottom: Cross-section; longitudinal section. Right top to bottom: Site plan; gallery-level plan.

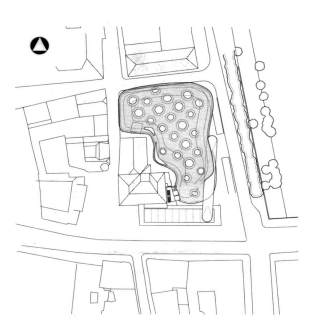

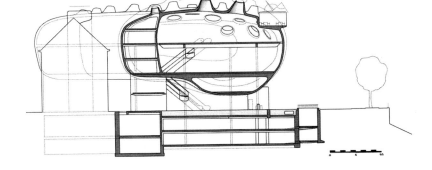

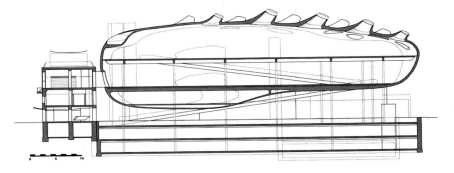

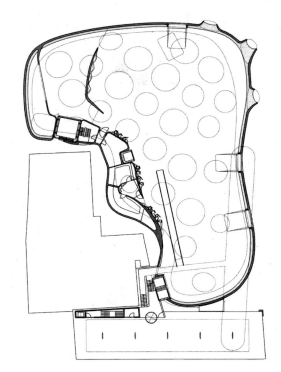

Left Concept sketch – the building is based on the fusion of two opposing ideas: the lightness of glass and the massive qualities of concrete.

Opposite The surface of the building is covered in panels of coloured aluminium that shimmer beneath the 16,000 square metres (172,200 square feet) of glass that forms the exterior sheath to the building.

Torre Agbar
Barcelona, Spain
2004

Architects
Jean Nouvel

Client
Layetana

Programme
Office headquarters
Public landscaped plazas

Location

Torre Agbar is located on a triangular site formed by the intersection of Calle Badajoz and the Avenida Diagonal. The two streets come together at an angle to form the grand Plaza de las Glòries in the Poble Nuo neighbourhood of Barcelona. Designed as the new headquarters for the society Aigües de Barcelona (AGBAR), the city's water company, the building is not only the tallest on Barcelona's skyline, but is also emblematic of the city's willingness to express its confidence in its own future – a tradition that came to the fore when it hosted the Olympic Games in 1992.

Site Description

The pedestrian approach to the building is via a route that offers views of the 'moat' that surrounds the base of the tower and the intriguing surrounding landscape. This ground plane suggests a lunar topography and features a 'mineral zone' forming a pit that disconnects the building from the ground plane, making it appear as if it has emerged fully formed from beneath the surface of the earth. A series of pools and cascades also adds to the creation of an intriguing public urban space. The ground-level entrance sequence comprises a bridge across a cleft that reveals the outer hull of the building passing downwards. This leads to a double-height entrance hall in which a cut-out with a descending staircase demonstrates the continuity of the inner core.

Building Solution

The Torre Agbar is based on the fusion of two opposing ideas: the lightness of glass and the massive qualities of concrete. Two non-concentric concrete cylinders rise up to the 26th floor, where a weightless dome of glass terminates the tower. The inner cylinder houses the stairs, services and lifts, while the space between the inner and outer ring is column-free open-plan office space. The outer cylinder, punctuated by 4,400 seemingly random window openings, is covered in panels of coloured aluminium that shimmer beneath the 16,000 square metres (172,200 square feet) of glass that forms the exterior sheath to the building.

The outer skin of the building consists of thousands of panes of glass, each measuring 1,200 by 300 millimetres (47 by 12 inches). The panels of glass, some transparent, others translucent, are fixed at varying inclinations over the entire surface of the building, acting as a technically sophisticated and aesthetically striking brise-soleil. The distribution of windows, apparently fortuitous, in fact responds to the orientation of the interior, so that offices facing south or west will have fewer openings than those situated on the north or east. Deep, lined reveals reflect diaphanous light into the interior, while the anodized-aluminium panels between the concrete and the glass provide back-lighting to the outer skin.

Thermal performance and the provision of natural light (not to mention spectacular views over the city), are achieved by combining the glass screen, the reflective metal and the thermal properties of the concrete to achieve an integrated environmental system that serves the whole building. Additional electricity is generated by solar cells on the building's surface, and the massive concrete perimeter walls act as a heat sink, smoothing out thermal ebbs and flows through the building fabric.

Between the core and the outer skin, the floors are lightweight decks on steel beams. The top six floors are pre-stressed reinforced-concrete plates cantilevered off the central core, and enclosed in a steel-framed dome. The two structural systems of concrete and steel are sheathed in the continuous screen of glass panels that curves

inwards and upwards to a recessed summit platform that conceals cleaning gantries and aerial walkways. The central core is capped off within the upper space, avoiding the usual lift overruns and plant rooms protruding from the top of the building.

The irregular curved form of the plan and the channel that surrounds the base of the tower accentuate the impression of a building that has risen up out of the ground to appear fully formed in the open space of the plaza. The simple concept of a building as an object brought into light is matched by the well-mannered form, striking but unimposing, an icon in the vibrant urban landscape of Barcelona.

Opposite, below and right The outer skin of the building consists of thousands of panes of glass, some transparent, others translucent, that are fixed at varying inclinations over the entire surface, and act as a technically sophisticated brise-soleil.

Below The distribution of windows responds to the orientation of the interior, so that offices facing south or west have fewer openings than those situated on the north or east.

Below right, far right and following pages Thermal performance and the provision of natural light are achieved by combining the glass screen, the reflective metal and the thermal properties of the concrete to achieve an integrated environmental system.

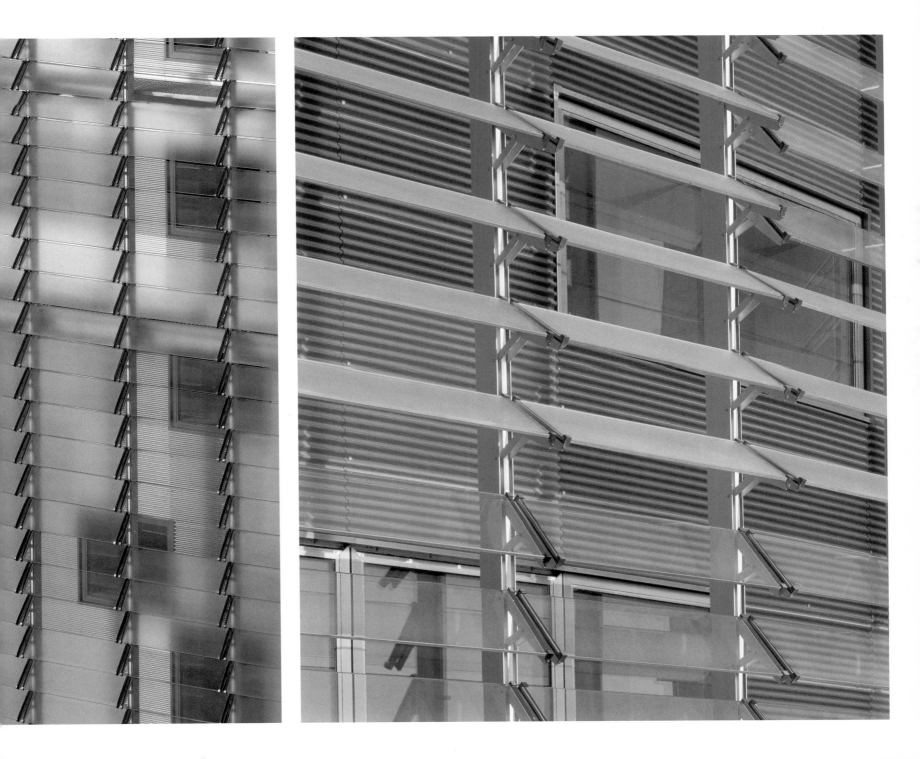

Opposite View of the building seen in the context of the surrounding low-rise structures that, until recently, characterized this part of Barcelona.

Below Left top to bottom: Section of Torre Agbar; section through the top of the tower. Right top to bottom: Site plan; high-rise floor plan; typical office plan.

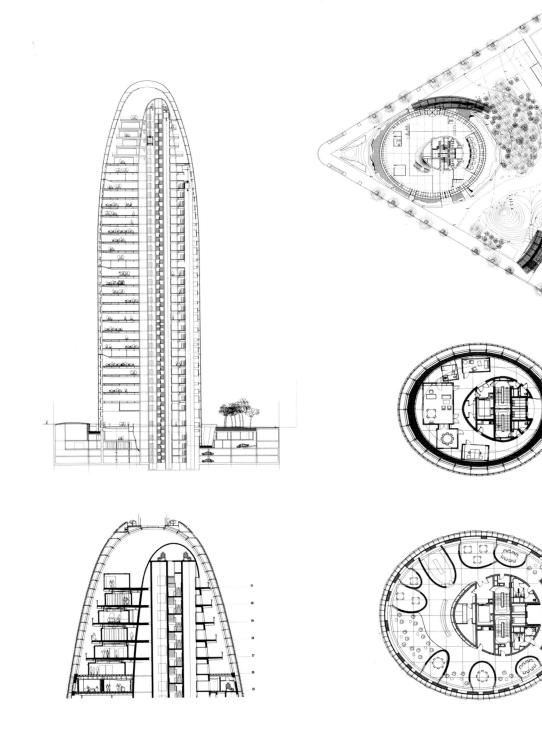

Project Credits

Kunsthaus, Bregenz, Austria
Architects
Atelier Peter Zumthor
Project Architects
Peter Zumthor, Daniel Büsser, Roswitha Büsser,
Katja Dambacher, Thomas Durisch,
Marlene Gujan, Thomas Kämpfer
Client
Land Voralberg

Shaw Offices, New York, USA
Architects
Steven Holl Architects
Project Architects
Steven Holl, Thomas Jenkinson,
Enge, Todd Fouser, Hideaki Ariizumi,
Adam Yarinsky, Annette Goderbauer
Mechanical and Electrical Engineers
Robert Derector Associates
Client
D. E. Shaw & Co.

**Kiasma Museum of Contemporary Art,
Helsinki, Finland**
Architects
Steven Holl Architects
Project Architects
Steven Holl, Vesa Honkonen, Justin Rüssli,
Chris McVoy, Janet Cross, Tomoaki Tanaka,
Pabo Castro-Estévez, Justin Korhammer,
Timothy Bade, Anderson Lee, Anna Müller,
Tapani Talo, Jan Kinsbergen, Lisina Fingerhuth
Associate Architect
Juhani Pallasmaa
Structural Engineers
Insinööritoimisto OY Matti Ollila & Co.
Consulting Engineers
Client
Finnish Ministry of Education/Museum of
Contemporary Art, Finnish National Gallery

Goetz Collection, Munich, Germany
Architects
Herzog & de Meuron
Project Architects
Jacques Herzog, Pierre de Meuron, Mario Meier
Associate Architect
Josef Peter Meier-Scupin
Structural Engineers
Behringer + Müller
Client
Ingvild Goetz

Fondation Cartier, Paris, France
Architects
Jean Nouvel/Emanuel Cattani & Associates
Project Architect
Didier Brault
Structural Engineer
Ove Arups & Partners
Client
Gan Vie, COGEDIM

Broadfield House Glass Museum, Dudley, UK
Architects
Design Antenna
Project Architect
Brent Richards
Structural Engineer
Dewhurst MacFarlane & Partners
Client
Metropolitan Borough of Dudley

The Museum of Art, Lille, France
Architects
Jean Marc Ibos/Myrto Vitart
Project Architect
Pierre Cantacuzene and Sophie Nguyen
Structural Engineer
Kephren Ingenierie
Client
Musée des Beaux Arts, Cité de Lille

Chapel of Ignatius, Seattle, USA
Architects
Steven Holl Architects
Project Architect
Timothy Bade
Associate Architect
Olson Sundberg Architects
Structural Engineer
Baugh Construction
Client
Seattle University

Concert Hall, St Pölten, Austria
Architects
Klaus Kada
Project Architects
Klaus Kada, Ursula Märzendorfer, Erwin Matzer,
Peter Rous, Willi Nakolnig, Heribert Altenbacher,
Alexander Forsthofer, Wolfgang Wimmer,
Frank Moritz, Robert Clerici, Ronald Schatz,
Herbert Schwarzmann, Elisabeth Kopeinig,
Claudia Schmidt, Michael Gattermeyer,
Ellen Kianek, Roswitha Küng-Freiberger,
Hubert Schuller
Client
NÖ Hypo Leasing Grundstücksvermietungs
GmbH

**Balearic Technological and European
Business Innovation Centre,
Majorca, Spain**
Architects
Alberto Campo Baeza Architects
Project Architect
Ignacio Aguirre, Anton Garcia Abril
Structural Engineer
Andres Rubio
Client
Government of Balearics/Juan de Austria Vial 'C'

**Museum Het Valkhof, Nijmegen,
The Netherlands**
Architects
UN Studio Architects
Project Architects
Ben van Berkel, Caroline Bos, Henri Snel,
Rob Hootsman, Remco Bruggink,
Hugo Beschoor Plug, Walther Kloet,
Marc Dijkman, Jacco van Wengerden,
Luc Veeger, Florian Fischer, Carsten Kiselowsky
Client
Nijmegen Municipal Council

**The Kursaal Centre,
San Sebastian, Spain**
Architects
Rafael Moneo Architects
Project Architect
Luis Rojo
Structural Engineer
NB35 Jesus Jimenez Canas
Client
City of San Sebastian/Diputacion
Foral of Guipuzcoa

**Great Court at the British Museum,
London, UK**
Architects
Foster & Partners
Project Architect
Sir Robert Smirke
Structural Engineer
Buro Happold
Mechanical and Electrical Engineer
Buro Happold
Client
British Museum

DZ Bank, Berlin, Germany
Architects
Frank Gehry & Partners
Project Architect
Randy Jefferson/Craig Webb
Structural Engineer
Jorg Schlaich Bergermann & Partner
Ingenieur Buro Muller Marl
Client
DZ Immobilien Management GmbH

Condé Nast Café, New York, USA
Architects
Frank Gehry & Associates
Project Architects
Frank Gehry, Randy Jefferson, Edwin Chan,
Christopher Mercier, Michelle Kaufmann,
Leigh Jerrard, Kamran Ardalan, David Nam
Associate Architect
Mancini Duffy
Client
Condé Nast Publications Inc.

Sendai Médiathèque, Sendai, Japan
Architects
Toyo Ito & Associates
Project Architect
Sejima Kazuyo /KT Architects, plus interiors by
Ross Lovegrove (UK) and Karim Rashid (US).
Structural Engineer
Mutsuro Sasaki
Client
City of Sendai

**Kimmel Center for the Performing Arts,
Philadelphia, USA**
Architects
Raphael Viñoly Architects
Project Architects
Raphael Viñoly, Jay Bargmann, Sandy McKee
Structural Engineers
Dewhurst Macfarlane with Goldreich Engineering
Client
Regional Performing Arts Center

Skywood House, London, UK
Architects
Graham Phillips
Project Architects
Graham Phillips, Simon Whiting
Structural Engineers
Ove Arup & Partners
Client
Graham Phillips and Diane Phillips

Colorium, Düsseldorf, Germany
Architects
Alsop Architects
Project Architects
Jonathan Leah, Uwe Frohmader, Christoph Egret,
Sonia Hibbs, Andy McFee, Niel Pusey,
Sabina Riss, Shaun Russell, Max Titchmarsh
Structural Engineers
Arup GmbH
Client
Ibing Immobilien Handel GmbH /Co.
Hochhaus KG

**City Hall, Alphen aan den Rijn,
The Netherlands**
Architects
Erick van Egeraat Associated Architects
Project Architects
Erick van Egeraat, Monica Adams,
Massimo Bertolano, Ralph van Mameren,
Harry Pasterkamp, Rowan van Wely, Jeroen ter
Haar, Colette Niemeyer, Ilse Castermans,
Matthieu Brutsaert, Ezra Buenrostro Hoogwater,
Jasper Jägers, Anke Schieman, Oliver von
Spreckelsen, Ronald Ubels, Jerry van Veldhuizen
Structural Engineers
ABT-C, Delft
Client
Municipality of Alphen aan den Rijn

Selected Bibliography

Laminata House, Leerdam, The Netherlands
Architects
Kruunenberg Van der Erve Architects
Project Architects
Gerard Kruuenberg and Paul Van der Erve + TNO
Industires Delft /Saint–Gobain Veenendaal
Structural Engineers
Van Rijn & Partners
Client
Leerdam Housing Association
(GWL Koopwoningen)

Laban Dance Centre, London, UK
Architects
Herzog & de Meuron
Project Architects
Jacques Herzog, Harry Gugger, Michael Casey
Structural Engineers
Whitby Bird & Partners
Client
Laban Centre

30 St Mary Axe, London, UK
Architects
Foster & Partners
Structural Engineers
Ove Arup & Partners
Client
Swiss Reinsurance Company

Kunsthaus, Graz, Austria
Architects
Spacelab Cook/Fournier
(Peter Cook and Colin Fournier)
Project Architects
Architektur Consult/Bollinger + Grohmann
Structural Engineer
Bollinger + Grohmann GmbH
Client
City of Graz/Kunsthaus Graz AG

Torre Agbar, Barcelona, Spain
Architects
Jean Nouvel
Project Architects
Jean Nouvel, Fermín Vázquez, Adriana Plasencia,
Ana Bassat
Associate Architect
+b720 Arquitectura
Structural Engineers
Obiol, Moya i Associats/Robert Brufau
y Asociados
Client
Layetana

Sophia & Stefan Glass Behling, *Glass: Structure and Technology in Architecture*, Prestel, New Jersey, 1999

Benito José, Rodriguez Cheda, Antonio Raya de Blas, *Tectonica 3 Glass(1)*

Jean Baudrillard, *The Singular Objects of Architecture*, University of Minnesota Press, Minneapolis, 2002

Jan Butterfield, *The Art of Light and Space*, Abbeville, New York, 1993

Dieter Bogner, *A Friendly Alien: Kunsthaus Graz*, Hatje Cantz Books, Cologne, 2004

Jean-Louis Cohen, *Le Corbusier*, Taschen, Cologne, 2004

Andrea Compagno, *Intelligent Glass Facades*, Birkhauser, Basel, 2002

Doreen Ehrlich, *Frank Lloyd Wright at a Glance: Glass*, BT Batsford, London, 2001

Richard Etlin, *Frank Lloyd Wright and Le Corbusier: The Romantic Legacy*, Manchester University Press, Manchester, 1994

Michael Freeman, *Space: Japanese Design Solutions*, Universe/Rizzoli, New York, 2004

Jeannine Fiedler, Peter Feierabend, *Bauhaus*, Könemann, Cologne, 2000

Mildred Friedman, Michael Sorkin, *Gehry Talks Architecture and Process*, Thames & Hudson, London, 1999

Todd Gannon, Jeffrey Kipnis, *The Light Construction Reader 2*, Monacelli Press, New York, 2002

Xavier Gonzalez, *A&T Layers*, Capas, 1988

Kristina Hartmann 'Sans un Pavillion de Verre' *L'Architecture d'Aujourd'hui*, 342, Sep–Oct 2002

Alan Hess, *John Lautner*, Thames & Hudson, London, 1999

Steven Holl, *Parallax*, Birkhauser, Basel, 2000

Steven Holl, Gerald Cobb, *The Chapel of St Ignatius*, Princeton Architectural Press, New York, 1999

Steven Holl, *In Search of Poetry of Thought, Matter, and Experience: Holl 1984–2000*, El Croquis, Barcelona, 2003

Alicia Imperiale, *New Flatness: Surface Tension in Digital Architecture*, Birkhauser, Basel, 2000

Philip Jodidio, *Alvaro Siza*, Taschen, Cologne, 2003

Conway Lloyd-Morgan, *Jean Nouvel: The Elements of Architecture*, Thames & Hudson, London, 1999

Jean Nouvel, *Jean Nouvel, Emmanuel Cattini & Assoc.* ICA/Artemis, London, 1992

Jean Nouvel, *Nouvel – The Symbolic Order of Matter*, El Croquis, Barcelona, 2002

Oscar Riera Ojeda, *Campo Baeza: Contemporary World Architects*, Rockport, 1997

Antonio Alberto Pizza, *Campo Baeza: Works and Projects*, Gustavo Gili, Barcelona, 1999

Henry Plummer, *Light in Japanese Architecure*, A+U Publishing, Tokyo, 1995

Franesco Proto, *Mass Identity Architecture – Architectural Writings of Jean Baudrillard*, Wiley, New York, 2003

Juan Carlos Rego, *Minimalism Design Source*, Harper Collins, New York, 2004

Brent Richards, *Space, Light, Phenomenal Transparency Detail – Building with Glass*, Sonderdruck, Aachen, 1998

Brent Richards, *Crystal Palace en Miniature*, InnoVerre, Saint Gobain, 1996

Dusan Riedl, *The Villa of the Tugenhauts*, Brno City Museum, Brno, 1997

Terence Riley, *Light Construction*, Gustavo Gili, Barcelona, 1996

Paul Scheerbart, John A. Stuart (translator), *The Gray Cloth – A Novel on Glass Architecture*, The MIT Press, Cambridge, 2003

Christian Schittich, *Building Skins: Concepts, Layers and Materials*, Birkhauser, Basel, 2001

Christian Schittich, Gerald Staib, *Glasbau Atlas*, Birkhauser, Basel, 1999

Norbert Schneider, *Vermeer: The Complete Paintings*, Taschen, Cologne, 2004

Gordon Strachen, *Chartres: Sacred Geometry, Sacred Space*, Floris Books, Edinburgh, 2003

James Turrell, *Air Mass*, South Bank Centre, London, 1993

Maritz Vandenberg, *Farnsworth House – Mies Van der Rohe*, Phaidon, London, 2003

Sarah Wigglesworth, 'La Maison de Verre ou la Modernite', *L'Architecture d'Aujourd'hui*, 342, Sept–Oct 2002

Michael Wiggington, *Glass in Architecture*, Phaidon, London, 1996

Ron Witte, *Toyo Ito: Sendai Médiathèque*, Prestel, New Jersey, 2002

Anatxu Zabalbeascoa, Javier Rodríguez Marcos, *Minimalism*, Gustavo Gili, Barcelona, 2000

Index

Acknowledgements

'Bright is the noble work; but, being nobly bright, the work should brighten the minds so that they may travel through the true lights …'
(Abbot Suger of St Denis, Paris, 1144)

For me the fascination with glass as a material has been a long one – it has been a literal revelation from understanding the material, to exploring the material qualities of glass, to finally seeking to reconcile the aesthetics of architecture using glass as a medium.

Despite its history, glass remains full of new possibilities in that it can capture architectural space and light, and can also reflect back the human context, and yet it is through the visible to the invisible that a state of consciousness is gradually realised. For Abbot Suger this was a spiritual journey that would lead to a mystical experience – an altered state of consciousness. For me, it has been a personal quest that appears to have no end, and continues to constantly transform my state of understanding. Many fellow contributors have affirmed this personal enquiry, but each has opened my eyes to see what I have not seen before, and allowed me to look beyond the immediacy of what I could see. They have nurtured my imagination and cultivated by thoughts, and made me realise the journey from the abstract requires extraordinary commitment and belief.

I am grateful that I have been able to contribute something to glass architecture in this book. Also, to build a glass pavilion in the heart of glass-making country (Broadfield House Glass Museum, Dudley, 1994) is my small homage to manifesting a future for glass architecture.

I would sincerely like the thank Tim MacFarlane of structural engineers Dewhurst MacFarlane, who were willing to understand my esoteric questions when I knew nothing and was a naive young architect, and who, over some 15 years, has been both a sure mentor and a professional consultant to my projects, and a good conveyor of principles and performance of glass.

I would also like to acknowledge the commercial support of Saint Gobain Glass/Solaglas, Friman Glass in my early works, and to Charles Hadjamach/Roger Dodsworth, Curators of Glass at Dudley for their enthusiasm, and Paul Watson of the borough of Dudley for being my first real client of a building in glass.

There have been many inspirations which, though not all experienced at first hand, have been undoubtedly instrumental in answering my desire for knowledge. From Paul Scheerbart for the inspiration of his visionary perceptions and dreams for glass architecture, to the presence of light in James Turrell's supreme works of coloured light, Marian Karel whose artistic glass works show a way to transformation architecture, Danny Lane for his simple insight of stacked and broken glass, Jean Nouvel for his realisation of the Foundation Cartier, Steven Holl for his 'emeshed experiences' in light architecture and Peter Zumthor for his profound understanding of materiality. But above all, to Terence Riley for his curation of the MoMA show in 1995, which contained the revelation for me of 'Light Construction', and to Colin Rowe/Robert Slutzky for their inspirational essay 'Transparency: Literal and Phenomenal', as well as to Eeva-Liisa Pelkonen and Rosemarie Haag Bletter for their essays, that have fundamentally crystallized and grounded my thoughts.

I would like thank Dennis Gilbert for his ongoing dialogue, whose sharp photographic eye has sought to translate my requests to crystallize architecture for this book. I would also like to acknowledge Catherine Slessor for her continued journalistic support of my buildings, my very patient publisher Philip Cooper of Laurence King, my editor Mark Fletcher, and Anna Mansfield for her fluid illustrations.

Above I am grateful to my family: Rosie (my partner), for putting up with my many hours spent writing into the night and at weekends, and to my children Paris, Beau and Elle, who have endured the piles of books that have adorned their environment as they have grown up around me.

Picture credits

All photographs are by Dennis Gilbert except for the following:

8	Yamaguchi Associates
16	Foto Marburg
17	Archipress/Franck Eustache
18 left	Peter Cook/VIEW
18 right	Nigel Young
20	Jean Nouvel
135-140	Christian Richters
143-149	Eduard Hueber/Arch Photo Inc.